Marriage
Annulment

Marriage Annulment

In the Catholic Church

Third Edition

Ralph Brown

Nihil Obstat
+ John Jukes O.F.M. Conv.
Auxiliary Bishop of Southwark
30 August 1990

Imprimatur
Basil Hume
Archbishop of Westminster
4 September 1990

Although all the examples given in this book are taken from actual cases, the names, places and dates have been altered to protect the participants' identities.

First published in Great Britain in 1990 by
Kevin Mayhew Ltd.,
Rattlesden, Bury St Edmunds,
Suffolk IP30 0SZ

© 1990 Ralph Brown

ISBN 0 86209 166 7

Typesetting and page creation by John Liffen
in association with B·E·P, Ipswich, Suffolk

Printed in Hong Kong by Colorcraft Ltd.

CONTENTS

PREFACE

THE FIRST edition of *Marriage Annulment* appeared in 1967. At that time the Second Vatican Council had only just finished, and the whole concept of development within the Church ('development' in Cardinal Newman's terms) was fresh upon us. Since that time things have moved fast. The documents implementing the practical teaching of the Council were published and took effect; and the process of revising the Code of Canon Law started and was finished; the Latin Code was translated into the vernacular; important studies were made in the jurisprudential understanding of marriage. During this time divorce by mutual consent was introduced in many countries; the divorce rate has spiralled; and (a new feature), the breakdown rate of second marriages following divorce has shot ahead of the rate for first marriage breakdowns; and in England, Ireland, Scotland and Wales, the number of cases brought before Ecclesiastical Marriage Tribunals multiplied by more than a factor of ten. In 1967, in some dioceses in the English speaking world, Marriage Tribunals did not – for all practical purposes – exist. Today it would be true to say that there is a network of Diocesan or Regional Tribunals throughout this area.

However, this increase in Tribunal activity could not justly be attributed to the Vatican Council. It had much more to do with the remarkable progress in the study of marriage, and the jurisprudential advances made by the Roman Rota dating from the 1940s. It was against this background that Tribunals moved into more effective action and there was a quickening of interest among lay persons about the Church's long-standing teaching on nullity and the dissolution of marriage. Another new departure was the training of religious and lay people in

Canon Law, and not only of priests as in the past. The Tribunals also started to make use of lay persons to assist in the handling of cases; and a further new development has been the increase in lay persons being trained and commissioned as evidence-takers.

It is probably now appreciated by most people that the role of the Marriage Tribunal is of enormous importance in the life of the Church. It is true that the manner of functioning of a Tribunal is, and must be, judicial. Nonetheless, as Pope John Paul II has pointed out, the chief purpose of the Tribunal procedure is to contribute to the pastoral aims of the Church, whether this means that some people can now marry in the Church, or have their unions recognised by the Church, or participate in the Sacraments, or even finally have their consciences quieted.

The Church's view of marriage has developed over the last twenty or so years, and much has been changed, added to or advanced, but the aim of the book remains the same: namely, to provide some reasonably accessible material for the benefit of priests in parishes, seminarians, parish Sisters, and people with their own marriage problems, and in general for the interested reader.

Deep personal thanks are due to professional colleagues and friends of long standing, especially Edward Dunderdale and Michael Ashdowne; Mrs Ivy Garnham who has soldiered through the text with her modern technology; Miss Barbara Nash and Miss Janet Smy who prepared the vital Index; and to the editor, John O'Hanlon. But, I am probably most of all indebted to the people I have met in connection with marriage cases, who have deepened my understanding of marriage and its jurisprudence, as well as having impressed me deeply with their bravery, courage, ability to laugh at adversity, and their genuine holiness in real-life situations often far stranger than any described in fiction. It is to these people that this book is really dedicated, with my thanks.

29th June, 1990   Monsignor Ralph Brown

Section I

MARRIAGE

Chapter One

DEVELOPMENTS IN PERCEPTION

*A*ND GOD said: It is not right that man should be alone. I shall make him a helper . . . and God made woman; and . . . this is why a man leaves his father and mother and becomes attached to his wife and they become one flesh' (Gen 2:18-24). Marriage is the first human institution noted in the scriptures; and this first institution launches into a history of development down through the centuries. Not that the nature of marriage itself has changed; what has developed is people's perception of marriage. This perception is still steadily developing today, and will undoubtedly continue to do so.

Marriage has been viewed very differently in all kinds of different societies in regard to rights, equality, relationships and all the rest. Views on the permanence of marriage, for example, changed very widely in the period up to the time of Jesus. Indeed Jesus commented on the fact that what was intended at the 'beginning' had been changed because of the 'hardness' of his listeners' hearts (Mk 10:5).

It is not within the scope of this book to analyse the scriptural arguments and meanings of this debate which Jesus had with the Pharisees. The point is to consider and illustrate the changes that have occurred in the understanding and treatment of marriage.

Although in the present, marriage is described as one of the seven sacraments, in fact marriage was not finally and universally accepted by the Roman Catholic Church as a saving sacrament in the Christian community until the 12th Century[1]. Of course, long prior to this the nature of marriage had been very thoroughly investigated by the Fathers of the Church and a great deal of writing is available from the first twelve centuries from such sources as St. Augustine, the mediaeval canonists, and especially in the debate between the University of Bologna and the University of Paris.

It must be understood that is was not the nature of marriage itself which was changing or developing, but the perceptions of scholars, theologians, canonists and many others. It was a question of, little by little, coming to recognise what was there; not changing what was there. Every age and change in society have brought their new insights into the understanding of marriage.

The same process is identifiable in the formal teaching of the Church in its Encyclicals, its Conciliar declarations and in its other Documents. The skill of the Church has been never to say too much too soon. Generally speaking, well aware of changing society and changing perceptions, the Church in its formal teaching has only really addressed a point here or a point there. For example, the Council of Trent *inter alia* addressed one particular detail concerning the celebration of marriage, because of a particular social problem that had arisen namely the need to prove the existence of a marriage. The description of marriage as such underwent development; the purposes of marriage were recognised more clearly as society and sciences progressed. The place and purpose of intercourse within marriage has of late been more carefully studied as there was a development in personalism as opposed to institutionalism. The place of 'relationship' in marriage is now more clearly understood.

A whole new light was thrown upon marriage by the Second Vatican Council in its teaching in the Constitution *Gaudium et Spes*, 'The Church in the Modern World', bringing with it the concept of marriage not merely as a contract, not only as a Sacrament, but as a community of life and love. Against this background it is to be expected that new patterns of thinking about marriage will have developed throughout the world. Obviously it would be quite untrue to suggest that all views and thinking about marriage have emanated from the Church's teaching. There will certainly have been a wide divergence of views amongst scholars around the world. Some of these views can in retrospect be seen as being very wide of the mark. It is always very difficult to assess a particular view and its consequences immediately and its consequences immediately and definitively. History and time allow for proper evaluation to take place; which is why it is so important that there is a *Magisterium*, a teaching Church, with the role of guiding and guarding.

It will of course be seen that the implications of all this development, as guided and guarded by the teaching Church, are very wide indeed. As the perception of what marriage is continues to develop, so of course does the perception of what marriage is not. For centuries the Church has had its Courts, or Tribunals, which have considered questions about the validity of marriage.

As a very simple example, the Church has taught from the 13th Century that the essence of marriage is the consent of the parties. Consequently, if it could be established that one of the parties had not given the required consent, then the union in question could not be regarded as a marriage. No-one actually invented consent as a necessary element of marriage; it was, eventually and after a long debate in the Church, perceived as an existing essential element. This is precisely where the development in the perceptions of marriage already noted have made possible the so-called developments in the Church's law in connection with nullity, or the dissolution of marriage.

One of the problems that will always be present is people's knowledge and understanding of what the Church teaches. For example, someone who was at school prior to the Second Vatican Council, and has not done much reading since, would probably be unaware of the insights already mentioned contained in that Council's document 'The Church in the Modern World'; and would therefore probably have no idea of the Church's teaching about marriage being a 'community of life and love'. Such a person would probably also have little idea of the Church's teaching on the 'discretion of judgement' required for two parties to marry validly. We need to appreciate that while at the heart of the work of the Church's Courts is the fact that marriage is an unchanging reality, society's perception of this reality does change.

If the perception and understanding of marriage are developing, it also stands to reason that the methods by which this reality is perceived should also change and develop. If, for example, it is necessary now to determine a person's psychological or psychiatric condition, then it is equally necessary for there to be an expert understanding of the human psyche. Training in the psychological and psychiatric fields is therefore necessary.

With the greater mobility and the speedier communications of the modern world, procedures need to be adapted, altered or changed to deal with these advances. With the huge increase in broken marriages over the last thirty or so years, there are bound to be many more persons seeking the assistance of the Church's Marriage Tribunals. Obviously, when fewer separated, there would have been fewer cases before the Church's Courts. The fact that the number of marriage cases or annulments granted has risen dramatically is not a sign of greater laxity; it is a sign of the need for competent, efficient and sound Tribunals to deal with the increase in cases.

But above all, if the Church does provide a service which examines broken marriages and determines whether such unions are marriages at all, then the people in the Church should be aware of this service and at least in general terms, how it operates. There is a need to appreciate that what is on the surface a marriage may for a very good reason eventually be determined never to have been a marriage. There is, of course, never any apportionment of blame or guilt in the conduct of a marriage case; but there must always be a careful examination and analysis of the reasons why such a union is not to be regarded as a valid and binding union.

The developments in the Church's view of marriage over the past forty years have been deeply significant; probably more so than in the previous two to three hundred years. There are a number of special reasons which can be pointed to as giving rise to such developments. The first is what may be referred to as Rotal jurisprudence (see page 18). We shall have further sight of practical examples of developments in jurisprudence later on in this book. These developments date in general from the nineteen forties. Jurisprudence could be described as case law; and one or two very particular areas of case law were specially developed in the late '40s and '50s. Until comparatively recently the reasons upon which a case was decided were only published ten years after they were given (this situation has now altered, and Rotal decisions are published much nearer the date that they were given). Apart from a few exceptions, such reasons for 'Sentences' as they are called of the 'forties and 'fifties only became available in the early 'sixties. It was therefore only then that these jurisprudential developments became available to the rest of the world. It was from these important decisions that the concept of 'the lack of due discretion' became apparent. From then onwards, a very great deal of work was done in the areas of personality disorder, psychopathy, hysteria, and generally in the field of psychiatric medicine.

A second great development in the understanding of marriage was the Second Vatican Council and the document already mentioned[2] This gave rise to a very considerable degree of study and writing, as well as further documents from the Holy See including *Humanae Vitae* of 25 July, 1968; and *Familiaris Consortio* of 22 November 1981.

A third special element in the development already discussed was the work on the revision on the Code of Canon Law. When Pope John XXIII announced the Second Vatican Council, at the same time he indicated that the changes which would inevitably be made by the

Council would call for the updating of the Code of Canon Law; and after the closure of the Council, Pope Paul VI established a whole set of procedures for this revision, which in fact took a little less than twenty years. During the period of this revision a great deal of work and study was deployed upon the sacrament of marriage; and considerable developments were studied, amended, honed and refined. This revision led to the promulgation of the New Code of Canon Law on 25 January, 1983; and it took effect from the First Sunday of Advent that year. The Code incorporated some extremely significant changes which reflected the developments already studied.

The last of the considerable influences on the developments made in this whole area concerns the great increase in marriage nullity work of the Church's Tribunals throughout the world. It has already been mentioned that the increase in this kind of work has largely derived from the unfortunate increase in marriage break-down; but that is not the only cause. Part of the increase in cases has been brought about by a concentration of effort in this direction; more training of Canon lawyers – priests and lay persons; a greater degree of study of problems associated with marital break-down; and more concentration on preparation for marriage, as well as counselling for those with marriage problems.

It may seem strange, but it is a fact that has been universally noted, that as local Tribunals began to increase in number and undertook more cases in regard to broken marriages, this invariably meant an increase in the number of cases presented. This has been noted throughout the world, and not only in countries where divorce exists. This increase in tribunal work has itself meant an increase in expertise; and this local expertise based especially on Rotal jurisprudence is another significant element in the development of the understanding of marriage. Incidentally, the insights about marriage as a relationship derived from counselling agencies, especially Catholic ones, have been immense.

The Growth of Common Law

It may appear strange but the Church never actually had a 'Code' of law until 1917. Of course it had laws, but no precise Code in the European sense of the term. From before the Middle Ages, laws in the Church tended to be local law, as legislated by a wide variety of provincial and other councils. These were councils held by bishops from a variety of districts, regions and provinces. There was some legislation at the major Councils of the Church such as the Council of Chalcedon and the four Lateran Councils. There were also a number of Apostolic Constitutions from the Popes. In the 12th Century a monk called Gratian collected together the great mass of ecclesiastical legislation from all sources. The real distinction of Gratian's collection was his attempt to put some kind of order into the legislation that had accumulated. This came to be called 'Gratian's Decree' (*Decretum Gratiani*) which was completed in approximately 1140, and became the basis for further collections. There were four great collections made between the time of Gratian and the Council of Trent which started in 1545: these collections, together with Gratian's decree, were now edited into a very large work called the *Corpus Juris Canonici*. This set of texts was then regarded as the law of the Church, together with all the other legislation from 1500 onwards, until the promulgation of the 1917 Code.

By the beginning of the 20th Century ecclesiastical law and legislation were an absolute jungle; and only the most learned of legal experts were able to find their way around and interpret the law. Consequently, in 1904, Pope St. Pius X gave instructions that a Code of Canon Law should be drawn up. This was done, and it was promulgated in 1917. It was subsequently replaced by the 1983 Code, which had been produced to take account of the changes in Church Law in general as a result of the Second Vatican Council.

There were some quite radical changes in the New

Code. But it must be noted that the bulk of these 'changes' had already been in operation long before the appearance of the New Code. Following the Council, in a large number of conciliar documents, changes had been called for. These changes were then enshrined in a variety of documents and the changes themselves implemented almost at once. Indeed changes that were called for at the very first session of the Council in the winter of 1963 were promulgated on a provisional basis on the 8th December of the same year. The New Code Law incorporates all these changes, and therefore it was already to some extent familiar when it was promulgated.

Jurisprudence

This brings us precisely to the distinction between the Code of Canon Law and the Church's jurisprudence. The latter term is one well known in English Law; there it broadly has the meaning of the philosophy of law. In canonical terms, the understanding of the term is very different. Here it has the meaning of 'case law'; that is the development of the law from case to case. However the significance of this is important. It is an established principle of Canon Law that no sentence or decision binds any other Court. The Code states quite clearly that: . . . an interpretation by way of a Court judgement . . . in a particular case, does not have the force of law. It binds only those persons and affects only those matters for which it was given (can.16,§3).

On the other hand 'case law', or jurisprudence in the canonical sense, is an extremely important, indeed invaluable guide for the interpretation of the law. It would be an irresponsible local Tribunal which did not take account of what the Rota had said on a particular matter. But all this is a matter of context. A judge in a local tribunal would obviously take account of what the Rota had said in a particular matter. On the other hand, it must be clear to a judge of a local tribunal precisely what the term 'Rotal

Jurisprudence' implies. The Roman Rota is divided into a series of panels, generally of three judges each; sometimes, in a specially important matter, there could be a panel of five judges. Presently the Roman Rota is divided into approximately seven such (three-judge) groups. The views of one of these groups would not necessarily be followed, or agreed with, by another group. It is really only by studying trends of the Roman Rota that a particular line might become apparent.

None of this, of course, means that in the Rota a particular marriage would be judged differently from one group of judges to another. The end decision would almost certainly be the same. What might well be different is the reasoning for the decision given, and it is the reasoning itself, not the actual decision, which creates the jurisprudence.

From this the difference between the Code of Canon Law and matrimonial jurisprudence will be apparent. However the nature and inner content of the difference need to be explained.

The Code of Canon Law is concerned with marriage in a variety of ways; although perhaps surprisingly not at any great length. It deals with the nature of marriage and the required consent; it deals with impediments to marriage; it deals with the preparation and various requirements for marriage; then the various procedures for examining the validity of a union; or determining the matter of baptism (or non-baptism) of the partners, as well as the assertion that a union was not consummated. It also, however, has a section which deals with various elements which would render a marriage null and void. These elements are what are termed the 'grounds' for nullity. Each one of these will be examined in detail later on. But for the sake of this chapter it will be useful briefly to mention grounds. It has already been stated that the Church decided a long time ago that what essentially 'made' a marriage was consent. Consequently, when grounds for nullity are dealt with in the code they are placed in the chapter dealing with 'Marital Consent'. Each ground concerns some aspect that would take away in whole or part or affect, the consent required to marriage.

Thus, for example, a person who goes through a cere-mony of marriage but does not *intend* to be married would give what is called simulated consent – that is, no real consent at all. A person who 'marries' solely with a view to assisting the other party to acquire British nation-ality and therefore to be allowed to remain in Britain, simulates consent. A person who enters marriage with the intention of not allowing his wife to have children; or with the reservation that he will part from his spouse and obtain a divorce if the relationship turned sour; or enters a union on the understanding that he retains a mistress – all these are forms of simulation because they take away from the full consent that is required for a persons to marry. Other elements which affect consent are error, ignorance, deceit, and force and fear. The Code of Canon Law sets out these and other elements which would be regarded as invalidating marriage, but they are not spelt out in any great detail.

This is precisely where the concept of ecclesiastical jurisprudence enters. It needs reiteration that the term is used in an entirely different sense to that used in English Law. In Canon Law it means explanation of the law by means of cases. Hence 'case law' would be one meaning of jurisprudence provided it is understood that a decision in one case does not bind a judge in another case. Case law in the canonical sense does not create precedent. Ref-erence has already been made above to the canon about the interpretation of the law. It will be recalled that while a nullity decision will affect this particular case, or these particular circumstances, it does not formally affect the general interpretation of the law.

When a Church Court gives a decision, or 'Sentence', in a marriage case, this first of all sets out a brief recital of the facts of the case and states the grounds alleged. The law is expounded in two principal parts; first of all, what the Code states the law to be on that particular ground; and then an examination of what current jurisprudence says about the particular area of study. The judge who writes the Sentence makes use of a variety of 'legal tools'. He explains the canonical understanding of the words used in the law of the Code; and he turns, for similar cases, to a wide selection of Rotal Decisions as well as the explanations given by the Decisions of local Tribunals; and he makes use of various articles or papers published in canonical journals written by experts in the law. If the case calls for it, he might also make use of clinical, medical and psychiatric expertise.

When this has been done, the third principal section of the Sentence applies this explanation of the law to the facts of the particular case in hand, and based on this jurisprudential background, explains the reasons why the judges in the case decided the matter the way they did. It is this corpus of legal explanation which is referred to in Canon Law as jurisprudence. When individual explanations of the grounds for nullity are given later on, they are based entirely on such jurisprudence.

The Courts and Tribunals

The functioning of a local Tribunal will be explained later, but it would be appropriate at this stage to explain the relationship between a local Tribunal, the Roman Rota and another Court called the *Segnatura Apostolica*. Firstly, it is necessary to state that a Tribunal (whether local or in Rome) is intended to deal with what are called 'criminal' cases: those which involve some ecclesiastical 'crime'. The Tribunal is also intended to deal with what are called 'contentious cases'; namely, those actions which arise between two parties on matters such as property rights and claims, or defamation *etc*; and the nullity of marriage and ordination. The subject of the present book concerns only a Tribunal in connection with marriage.

In each Diocese or Region there is a Tribunal which deals with marriage cases. In some countries, England and Wales for example, there are Diocesan Tribunals; in others (Ireland and Scotland) there are Regional Tribunals. However, this distinction is merely for the sake of administrative ease. Since almost always there is an appeal against a decision given in the I Instance, every Tribunal has an established Appeal Court or 'Tribunal of II Instance'.

In Rome there is a special Tribunal called the Roman Rota. This, in the main, acts as a Court of Appeal for cases sometimes in the II Instance from Tribunals around the world (that is, an appeal can be made from the Tribunal of I Instance direct to the Roman Rota); or more often in the III Instance, if a case goes that far. The Roman Rota also deals with certain other cases, but these need not detain us here.

In Rome there is also a Tribunal called the *Segnatura Apostolica*. The ramifications of most of its work are not relevant here; but what is relevant is that the Segnatura has a special role of vigilance over the local Tribunals of the world. Sometimes it may be necessary in special cases to apply to the *Segnatura* for various permissions or guidance.

However, from all this, it will be apparent that the bulk of marriage cases around the world are dealt with locally; and not in Rome. For this reason, therefore, the bulk of the contents of this book relates to the work of local Tribunals.

1 Macklin, *What is Marriage* New York, 1982, p.31.
2 The Apostolic Constitution: 'The Church in the Modern World' *Gaudium et Spes*, nn. 47-57.

Chapter Two

MARITAL CONSENT

THE CATHOLIC Church teaches that a valid, sacramental and consummated union is indissoluble. Such has been the Church's teaching for centuries. What this means is that two baptised persons, who are married in accordance with the law, and whose union has been consummated , are bound in an indissoluble union sanctified by God until the death of one of the partners. This applies equally to Catholics and non-Catholics. The only additional law to which Catholics must conform, is the rule that, without a special dispensation, those baptised in the Catholic Church must be married before a priest and two witnesses. This additional rule is termed the 'form of marriage' and applies throughout the Latin Church, but for special reasons it can be dispensed. With such a dispensation, a Catholic is permitted to contract marriage validly and lawfully in a church, and before the minister, of another Christian denomination: the situation of a member of the Orthodox Church will be dealt with later. The teaching that a valid, sacramental and consummated union is indissoluble until death applies even to a marriage between two non-Catholics wherever that takes place.

It is often thought, by Catholics and non-Catholics alike, that the Church does not recognise a marriage which takes place in a Register Office. As mentioned above, this is not the case. Apart from the case of Catholics, who are bound to the 'form of marriage', a marriage can, canonically, take place anywhere. The Church teaches that what makes a marriage is the full consent of the partners. Assuming that consent has been given by both the parties to a marriage, the union is valid.

Moreover, assuming that this same union is also sacramental and consummated, it is indissoluble.

It will be seen that the Church stresses the three elements of an indissoluble union, namely, validity, sacramentality and consummation. But, although a union which enjoys these three elements is indissoluble, it also follows that a union which does not possess these three qualities may be declared not to be marriage, or at least in certain circumstances, may be dissolved by the Church.

The work of a Marriage Tribunal centres around the determination of these three elements; whether the marriage is invalid; whether it is non-sacramental; whether it is unconsummated. The next few pages will be devoted to an examination of what is meant by these three terms.

Validity

For a considerable period in the history of the Church there was a dispute as to precisely what 'made' a marriage. In the late Middle Ages, there were those, principally, of the Law School of Bologna, who maintained that it was consent followed by intercourse which made the marriage. The other view, that of the Law School of Paris, held that it was simply consent here and now in the present to be man and wife which created a true marriage. Eventually this dispute was resolved by the scholar who became Pope Alexander III (1159-1181) in his celebrated work called: 'The Sentences' written just before he was elected Pope. Alexander declared for the Parisian view, namely consent alone. This was confirmed by Pope Urban III (1185-1187), and subsequently by Pope Innocent III (1198-1216).

A Christian marriage involves a union 'which has been established by God and qualified by his laws. It is rooted in the conjugal covenant of irrevocable personal consent. Hence, by that human act whereby the spouses mutually bestow and accept each other, a relationship arises by the Divine Will which, in the eyes of society too is a lasting one.'[1] This description of marriage is deeply impressive; it is couched in language which is pastoral and real, rather than dry and legal. Nonetheless, the description contains a number of very precise notions which must be highlighted here. Irrevocable personal consent is given by the two parties to a union involving a relationship between them which is lasting and permanent. There is a mutual giving or exchange which involves the couple in a permanence that is foreseen and strengthened by the Divine Will. The clear meaning here is that this union, forged by the consent of the parties, is irrevocable – 'until death do us part'.

In addition, the same conciliar document goes on to state that 'By their very nature, the institutions of matrimony and conjugal love are ordained for the procreation and education of children . . .'[2] The Council here is stating nothing more than that one of the purposes of the conjugal state is the children that may come forth from the union. But there is no compulsion about having children; merely a statement that this is one of the purposes of the bond. This portion of the text must be taken together with the one mentioned earlier, both of which underline that there is a free giving of consent, an exchange, to a union which in no way excludes the possibility of children. It is also implicit here that each of the parties, as a result of the consent freely given and accepted, is entitled to be a parent.

The Constitution continues: 'Thus a man and woman who, by the marriage covenant of conjugal love "are no longer two, but one flesh", render mutual help and service to each other in an intimate union of their persons and of their actions . . . As a mutual gift of two persons, this intimate union, as well as the good of the children, imposes total fidelity on the spouses and argues for an unbreakable oneness between them.'[3] The teaching here is that the married state, because of the consent given by the parties to each other and because of their rights to children, also imposes upon the couple the obligation of total fidelity so as to safeguard the union and the children of the union.

These conciliar writings, which presented the Church's universal teaching on marriage, were then taken up in the New Code of Canon Law, promulgated in 1983. The part of the Code which reproduces the teaching in legal form is at the beginning of the section which deals with consent (cann. 1055-1057; and can. 1101, §1).

Marriage is made by the consent of the parties – in a meeting of minds and wills of the parties; the meeting of minds regarding marriage in its proper understanding. Logically, therefore, where there is an absence of the understanding or the will, there is no consent, only an outward manifestation.

Consent, put it as its simplest, has two central aspects. One consents *to* something; and one consents *with* something. The something *to* which one consents is called the 'object of consent'; and what one consents *with* are those powers and personal requirements which allow one to consent to the object. The object of consent is marriage as taught and explained by the Church. The Church describes marriage as a 'covenant' between a man and a woman; this covenant establishes a partnership for whole life; and the partnership is directed towards the well-being of the spouses as well as the procreation and upbringing of children (can. 1055, §1). The essential properties of marriage as taught by the Church are its unity and indissolubility. (can.1056). Finally, the Church also teaches as well as stating it in the law, that marriage between the baptised has been raised by Christ to the level of sacrament. (can. 1055, §1).

So much for the object of consent. Now to give consent one needs certain powers and attributes. These must, of course, not be over-pitched because marriage is a natural state; and a person cannot be required to possess examination degrees to enter it; or to put it another way, the person only needs to be qualified by the university of life. Thus it is utterly reasonable, as well as necessary, that a person should be of a marriagable age; it will be seen as most unjust that a person should be forced into marriage, either by means of physical or moral force or fear exerted, or by ignorance of the nature of marriage, or deceived by an error about the other party. The person needs, obviously, to be sane and possessed of a degree of judgemental ability to decide upon marriage; as well as to have at least a minimal ability to form and sustain the partnership of which the Code speaks. All these points about the object of consent and the nature of consent are precisely the areas of investigation by a Marriage Tribunal in regard to validity.

The quotation from the conciliar document 'The Church in the Modern World' already given, re-states that marriage has been established by God and is qualified by his laws. When Christ founded his Church, he committed into the hands of Peter and the Apostles the guardianship of the sacraments within the Church. It is from this that the Church derives its power to legislate about the sacraments and to establish certain laws concerning the existence and contracting of marriage. Certain laws of the Church on marriage are of the greatest importance. Some of these are called Divine Laws, because it is considered that they have been established by God, and are therefore merely re-stated by the Church. Other laws have been made by the Church; and these are called Ecclesiastical Laws. Thus, some laws prevent a marriage taking place; for example, it is not possible for a boy to marry his mother or his sister. Such prohibitions are considered to be of the Divine Law. Another law, usually regarded as being of ecclesiastical origin, forbids two first cousins to marry. When the laws which the Church has either re-stated from the Divine Law or formulated as Ecclesiastical Law, prohibit marriage either absolutely or less severely, such laws are termed impediments. Impediments of the Divine Law cannot be dispensed by the Church; consequently, a marriage which takes place in spite of the existence of such an impediment is regarded as null and void. Impediments of Ecclesiastical Law can be dispensed by the Church; but if a marriage takes place without a dispensation, it would be regarded as invalid.

A Marriage Tribunal is concerned with all these impediments. Generally speaking, the matters which concern consent, or the lack of it, are dealt with by what is termed a *formal nullity procedure*. Other matters concerning impediments and whether they have been dispensed or not, are usually dealt with under the heading of an *informal nullity procedure*. For the present, it is merely stated that matters concerning consent and impediments are the subject of *nullity cases*.

Sacramentality

In speaking about the married state, the Constitution 'The Church in the Modern World' says: 'Authentic married love is caught up into divine love and is governed and enriched by Christ's redeeming power and the saving activity of the Church. This love can lead the spouses to God with powerful effect and can aid and strengthen them in the sublime office of being father or mother.' The married state is being described here as a means by which a couple can fulfil their destiny as planned by God, and that they will go to God through their life in the married state. The constitution continues: 'For this reason, Christian spouses have a special sacrament by which they are fortified and receive a kind of consecration in the duties and dignity of their state.'

For centuries, the Church has taught that marriage is a sacrament. Moreover, the theology of the sacrament shows that marriage is one sacrament shared by both the spouses and not two sacraments, one for each. It is a sacrament of unity for the couple, a sacrament which draws them closer to God. From this it is evident that there can only be one sacrament of marriage. There cannot be only a part of a sacrament – it is either there or not there. Then again, it is part of the Church's teaching that to be able to receive other sacraments it is necessary first to be baptised; that is, to have been admitted into the

Christian community. Consequently, it follows that for a couple to be able to receive the Sacrament of Matrimony, it is necessary that both the parties are baptised, and are members of the Christian community.

From this it will be seen that a marriage will be a sacrament when both the parties are baptised. Conversely, although the couple may be genuinely holy and receive enormous gifts from God, their marriage cannot be regarded publicly as a sacrament if one or both have not been baptised. On the other hand, if both parties are baptised into the Church, even after their marriage has been celebrated and the couple is still together, their existing marriage thereby becomes a sacrament. It should be stressed at this point that although a marriage may not be a sacrament, it is nonetheless assumed to be valid and binding. The couple who are parties to a non-sacramental union are still naturally bound to a permanent union.

However, the teaching of the Church maintains that the Pope has power, which he can exercise in very special circumstances, to dissolve a non-sacramental union which has already broken down.

This power of the Pope is often referred to as the 'Petrine Privilege' called such as an extension of the 'Pauline Privilege'. This latter has its authority in St Paul's First Letter to the Corinthians, (1 Cor 7:8-13). In this Letter, Paul warns the Corinthians, still living in a pagan world, that after becoming converted to Christ, it might happen that the convert's married partner remains a pagan and refuses to live in peace without offence to the Creator. In such circumstances the Christian party was given permission to leave the pagan partner, so as to be able to lead a full Christian life. Such a Christian was also given permission by St Paul to remarry, and it is the teaching of the Church that the first marriage is dissolved in the act of exchanging consent in the second union. The details of both the Pauline and the Petrine privileges will be considered in Chapter 9. It is sufficient to note here that where a marriage is not a sacrament, it lies within the power of the Holy Father to dissolve this union in certain special and restricted circumstances.

Consummation

The Constitution 'The Church in the Modern World', urges couples to nourish and develop their wedlock by conjugal love and undivided affection. It continues: 'This love is an eminently human one since it is directed from one person to another through an affection of the will . . . This love the Lord has judged worthy of special gifts: the healing, perfecting, and exalting gifts of grace and charity. Such love, merging the human with the divine, leads the spouses to a free and mutual gift of themselves, a gift proving itself by gentle affection and by deed . . . This love is uniquely expressed and perfected through the marital act'.[4]

We have already mentioned the conflict which arose between the Law Schools of Paris and Bologna as to whether marriage was *made* by consent or by consummation. It had long been held before this debate that a valid sacramental marriage which had already been contracted was rendered indissoluble when it was consummated, since this act was taken to be a symbolic representation of the union between Christ and his Church. Conversely, it was argued, that where a marriage had not yet been consummated, it was at least theoretically dissoluble because it did not yet bear the seal of the union of Christ with his Church. As in so many other matters, what appears to have determined the teaching of the Church was the actual practice of the Church. Although there were certain periods during the Middle Ages when some Popes did not allow dispensations to be granted in favour of remarriage when the original union had not been consummated, it was a slowly growing practice to allow this dispensation in certain closely defined circumstances.

It is indeed part of the teaching of the Church that if a

sacramental and valid union had not been consummated, it is at least theoretically possible for the union to be dispensed. Some of the historical development of this practice and the rules relating to it will be discussed later in Chapter 8 (the Code of Canon Law deals with the matter of non-consummation at can.1061, §1 and cann.1697-1706). At this stage, it is merely noted that the Church does grant such dispensations and it is therefore part of the work of the Tribunal, acting on behalf of the Holy See, to assemble indications and proofs that the marriage in question had not been consummated.

Lack of Form

It has already been shown that the Church regards itself as competent to legislate about the administration and celebration of the sacraments. One of the stipulations which the Church makes about marriages which involve at least one Catholic is that a certain 'form' should be observed. It is necessary for such a marriage to be celebrated before a priest in a Catholic Church and before two witnesses. If such form is not dispensed, and a union takes place without observing this form, the Church regards that union as invalid; for example, a baptised Catholic who marries in a Register Office or in a non-Catholic Church. The law has a special procedure for dealing with such cases which will be examined later.

Illegitimacy

Many people who might be involved in nullity cases tend to draw back or refuse to co-operate because of the fear that a Decree of Nullity would mean that the children born of the union would be regarded as illegitimate. This, in fact, is a needless fear. The law of the Church has always made it clear that a union subsequently declared null and void is regarded by the Church as 'putative', provided that it was celebrated in good faith by at least one of the parties. It would not be regarded as putative when both the parties were certain of its nullity. The children of a putative marriage are considered to be legitimate. However, it will be noted, that in ordinary circumstances a couple can only be certain that their union was null and void when it has been so declared by the Church; and for the Church to do this the couple would have already been separated and divorced. Hence there is no chance of the children of such a union ever being regarded as other than legitimate. In any event, for all ecclesiastical and spiritual purposes, illegitimacy has no effect on the persons, whatever may be the civil situation according to the local civil law.

Bereavement

This may be regarded as a strange term to use in the context of Tribunal work on nullity cases, when evidently both parties must be alive. However, bereavement does not merely refer to the situation of the surviving relatives after a physical death. Bereavement involves any loss; and, of course, a broken marriage is an example of profound traumatic loss. It is true that where there has been a really terrible marriage perhaps the only apparent (at least the first) reaction is relief for, say, the wife and children. But although there may well be relief at the termination of such a union, the events leading up to it must have been extremely traumatic.

As with any trauma, or shock, there is always a reaction which is generally quite profound. One of the problems of the present social pattern is speedy remarriage after a break-down. This usually means the person in question never adequately externalises all the sadness, bitterness, guilt and the rest which have built up beneath the surface. Present statistics show that in general there is a higher break-down rate in second marriages than there is in first marriages. The reasons are not hard to find. The second chosen partner frequently resembles the first. The un-externalised feelings have not been sorted out; the person has not yet come to terms with himself or herself.

The Church's nullity procedure is not just a form of Church divorce. A fairly considerable time elapses between the break-down of the marriage and the commencement of nullity proceedings, which in any event are usually only formally started when a divorce decree absolute has been granted. The section on procedure will demonstrate what must take place in a nullity case; but generally, the observation of all the required procedures will involve on average something between twelve to eighteen months; and it might be even longer.

Although there is nearly always a great deal of anxiety in the petitioner and an urge to speed matters, such speed is not an advantage so far as a second union is concerned. The nullity procedure involves lengthy statements, formal evidence, probing questions. By the end of a successful procedure the petitioner usually feels that the time taken has provided a bereavement period, which has allowed the person to come to terms with the innate feeling of guilt and failure. Most Tribunals are able to produce letters of thanks from petitioners at the end of their cases which dwell specifically on this need to have come to terms with the feeling of failure. The fact that failure as a concept or feeling may not be uppermost in a person's mind at the time of break-down and divorce, does not take away from the fact that it is a principal human emotion which is built into the sub-conscious. The nullity procedure helps this problem in a very positive fashion.

However, in addition to this very practical point about bereavement, it must also be noted that a Tribunal is dealing with something that might be a sacrament, or at least a valid union. The care required by the Church in its procedures is only a reflection that the nullity and other procedures are not divorce by agreement; and that when the Church has issued a decree of nullity or a dissolution or a dispensation, it is morally certain that no-one has tampered with 'what God has put together'.

It has been the aim of the chapter to describe the concept of consent – the field within which the Marriage Tribunal works. Cases involving nullity, dissolution, or dispensation, will all be dealt with in subsequent chapters. It will already have been seen, however, that the scope of the Tribunal is by no means confined to the nullity of marriage. Therefore, in the following chapters, in addition to an examination of the grounds for nullity, and the formal judicial procedure, we will also deal with non-consummation and non-baptism cases, describing something of the historical background and covering the requirements of the modern-day process.

1 Pastoral Constitution of the II Vatican Council: *The Church in the Modern World* para. 48.
2 *ibid. loc. cit.*
3 *ibid. loc. cit.*
4 *ibid* para 49

Section II

INVALID MARRIAGE

Chapter Three

SIMULATION OF CONSENT

A MARRIAGE can be declared null and void either if there was no consent given to the marriage, or if the consent was in some way defective. Each of the grounds will now be examined.

Total Simulation

Put at its simplest, total simulation means that person apparently consents to a marriage, and all that it stands for, but actually does not. Initially it may sound strange that a person can apparently enter into the solemn state of marriage with the intention of not getting married! But, in fact, of course, it does happen; and when consent is completely withheld, the union is null and void. This is termed simulated consent or total simulation. However, it is not sufficient to allege this was the case; it must be proved by means of evidence that despite all the signs to the contrary, the person was actually and completely intending that the marriage would not be the outcome of the action performed, usually in a church and in front of a congregation: such evidence comes from witnesses; that is, persons who knew from some source, that the consent had not been given. It will immediately be clear that such evidence is not always easy to find.

The law of the Code stipulates that any apparent marriage is presumed to be valid until the contrary is proved. That is precisely what the witnesses must be able to do; namely, make sworn statements to the effect that the consent was going to be withheld; and then produce witnesses, or at least circumstantial evidence, showing that *de facto* consent in the event was withheld. The allegation of the party or parties, or the mere opinions of witnesses, are not sufficient. The simulation must be established by means of irrefutable evidence.

There is a further general difficulty which arises in any nullity case. When a marriage has turned out badly, little by little, a person, without any intention to lie or deceive, can come to think that he did not give consent at the outset, or that his consent was defective in some way. Innocent, though real, self deception is always a problem; and this is one of the reasons why proof from external sources is required.

A person can, of course, allege his own lack of consent as a ground for nullity. He may have been in a situation of serious pressure, not sufficient for force and fear, but sufficient to make him go through the external celebration of the marriage. The confusion and the pressure may have combined to remove all possibility of guilt: nonetheless, until the facts have been made clear, the judges are bound to treat the allegation with great caution.Such caution can, however, be overcome if there are unimpeachable witnesses who knew the facts; or if there is some kind of documentary evidence. Of course, the judges in such a case must always be wary of documentary evidence, or at least certain kinds of documentary evidence. The problem is to ensure that such evidence pre-existed the marriage. Falsified documentary evidence is not unknown to the Church's Marriage Tribunals. It may be noted here that there is a growing custom amongst some civil lawyers who represent wealthy clients, to suggest that a document is drawn up prior to a marriage which commits the parties to a particular kind of distribution of property should the marriage break down. This kind of documentary evidence, however, properly belongs to our consideration later on of the exclusion of permanence (see page 51).

Although, by the nature of the case, proof of total simulation is difficult to find, such grounds are not impossible to prove. The jurisprudence of the Marriage Courts of the Church ordinarily demand four basic requirements for such grounds to be established. What these requirements amount to are 'indications of proof'.

• Firstly, it is necessary that there is some statement made by the person who simulated the consent. If the person concerned made a statement admitting the simulation just after the wedding ceremony, and there is a witness to testify to this, such evidence is extremely important.

• Secondly, some reasonable explanation is required for the simulation. Reasonable explanation of the simulation might be the circumstances in which the person was brow-beaten into marriage, or where strong pressure existed, or even grave fear.

• Thirdly, the jurisprudence of Marriage Tribunals demands that the circumstances surrounding the marriage point towards simulation as a possibility – for example, if a man deserted his wife directly after the wedding and disappeared; or where he stated to other people after the ceremony that it had been a farce because he had not intended to marry.

• Finally, as in all cases, the evidence is required of persons other that the parties, who can support and confirm the statements and allegations made by the principals.

Examples of Total Simulation

Sonia and Henry

Henry *was a young unmarried executive who had recently joined an important firm; due to his good work he had come to the very welcome notice of the Chairman of the Board. An invitation to the Chairman's house followed, where Henry met the daughter, **Sonia**. Initially he was attracted to her and she responded; but as he got to know her better he found her to be spoilt, domineering and, with other young men, flirty. Henry's position in the Company advanced, and he showed great promise. Sonia's mother took a hand and decided that Henry would be a suitable marriage for Sonia. The mother was even more*

39

domineering than the daughter, and she began making plans for an engagement and then the wedding. Henry, meanwhile, had met another girl, **Belinda**, much more to his liking and these two fell in love. But try as he would, he sensed that he was becoming more and more committed to marry Sonia; not because of any liking for her, but because of the mother; and specially because the latter had subtly, but nonetheless clearly, indicated that unless he did marry Sonia, his position in the Company would be in jeopardy. Not of strong character, he felt trapped and found himself leading two lives. He did not dare tell Sonia about Belinda because he was convinced the mother would create havoc. He did not dare tell Belinda, whom he truly loved, about Sonia lest this should spoil their relationship. Very clearly he showed his own family that he was deeply opposed to the marriage with Sonia, but he felt he could not endanger his career. He contrived with some igenuity to see Belinda right up until the day before the marriage; wrote to her three times from the honeymoon hotel; and, of course, very soon the marriage with Sonia collapsed, and he went to live with Belinda. Not long afterwards, Sonia petitioned for a decree of nullity on the grounds of Henry's total simulation, and on the basis of evidence from Henry himself, Belinda, Henry's parents and Sonia's mother, a decree of nullity was issued.

Peter and Mary

Peter and **Mary** were only 17 when they first went out with each other. Mary had been adopted and she had not had a happy home life with her adoptive parents. She and her adoptive mother never got on well; and Mary somewhat unjustly blamed her unhappiness on the fact that this was not her own mother. When the two youngsters had been going out for some time, intercourse took place; but already Mary's interest in Peter was waning. Shortly afterwards they parted. Then Mary discovered she was pregnant. She got in touch with Peter and they decided to tell their parents. The two sets of parents were upset, but extremely kind and understanding. They felt that the two were somewhat young and immature for marriage, but said that whatever they decided they would stand by the youngsters; and if Mary decided not to marry, the adoptive mother would help her and the baby. To everyone's surprise (knowing by now that Mary had tired of Peter's attentions), Mary announced that she was going to marry him. There did not seem to be any warmth or affection in this announcement; nor did she show any towards Peter. She merely insisted that she was going to marry him. With some anxiety the parents allowed the marriage to take place; and it turned out to be a disaster.

Mary did not want intercourse with Peter, though it did in fact take place a couple of times against her will. She made clear to Peter that now the marriage had taken place, he could do what he liked; as for her, she was going to remain with him until after the baby was born, and then return to her parents. Argue as he might, Peter could not move her; and indeed after the birth of the baby she did return to her parents for a while and then shortly afterwards left them to set up house on her own with the baby. Peter petitioned for a decree of nullity on the grounds of Mary's simulation. Good and convincing evidence was brought to show that Mary's whole mind had been to go through a ceremony of marriage with the father of the baby, so as to be able to produce a legitimate certificate of birth for the baby, but apart from that she was not interested in marriage or Peter at all. A decree of nullity was granted.

Fiona and James

Fiona, a young and attractive student from South Africa, 20 years of age, had come to England to study ballet. She enrolled in her ballet school and was given Home Office permission to remain in the country for two years, for the duration of her studies. This would have been sufficient

41

for the particular course that she had undertaken to follow; but unwisely, as it turned out, she also did four short two-month courses at various cultural centres in Europe. By the end of the two-year permitted residence period, she had not completed her training, and was threatened with expulsion from the country under the regulations governing overseas students.

She had a girlfriend at College who said that she knew a young man, **James**, who was English, and was studying to be a doctor, but still had four years of his training to go. He was a friendly and obliging fellow; and he might agree to marry Fiona and thereby allow her to acquire British nationality. After two years a divorce could be applied for, and then both would be free, and Fiona could remain in England. The proposal was put to James and so far as he was concerned, he was busy studying; he had no romantic attachments; he would not qualify for another four years; he would be affected in no way at all by undertaking such a proposal.

The couple gave notice to the Registrar and in due course they went through a Register Office union with two friends acting as witnesses. They came out of the Register Office, had a drink together, and then went their separate ways. He did not live with her; there was no intercourse; and the next time the couple met as a few weeks later so as to acquire a passport for Fiona. The next time they were in contact was to arrange the divorce. `Leaving aside the moral and legal considerations of these facts, they clearly established the invalidity of the union by reason of total simulation. Of course, any Tribunal must strongly disapprove of this devious conduct; but when at length such a case is presented to a Tribunal, the only point at issue for the tribunal itself is whether the union in question is null and void or not. It will also be noted that this kind of case can only arise in the situation of two non-Catholics since a Register Office marriage for a Catholic would in any event have been invalid by reason of defect of form.

It will be noted at once that there is a fundamental difference between these three cases. In the first case Henry did not want to marry Sonia, and if he had dared he would have run a mile from the situation. Thus equivalently when he was saying the worlds at the altar: 'I do' and 'I will', his mind was stating the complete reverse, 'I don't' and 'I won't'. On the other hand, in the second case, Mary was adamant that she was going to get married; and no-one was going to stop her; and yet that too is regarded as simulation. In the third case, both Fiona and James wished to go through a ceremony of marriage, but intending that the end product would simply be Fiona's British Passport. The jurisprudence of the Church has long perceived that a person may wish to go through a *form of marriage* and yet at the same time not wish to enter into the *state of marriage*. In Mary's case the only way in which a document could be obtained to show that her baby was legitimate was by going through a form of marriage; and thereafter she showed no interest whatsoever in Peter. In the case of Fiona and James, Fiona's continued residence in England would be allowed only by means of the possession of a British Passport; there was no interest whatsoever in marriage apart from that. Thus the fundamental similarity, apart from the superficial differences, between these three cases, is that neither Mary, nor Henry, nor Fiona, nor James intended to enter into the married state as understood by the Church. Where it can be shown that the person in question had excluded lifelong union, but had nonetheless gone through a ceremony of marriage, the grounds of total simulation are satisfied.

Partial Simulation

The manner in which the law of the Church now expresses itself on the matter of consent has already been seen in its totality, when dealing with the complete denial of consent, or total simulation. The law also indicates that the essential properties of marriage are its unity and

43

indissolubility; and an essential element of marriage is its ordering to the well-being of the spouses and the procreation and up-bringing of children. These properties constitute what might be described as the *object of consent*; that is, what the parties are consenting to. Of course, they are consenting to a very much wider array of qualities in marriage, a marriage relationship, a community of life and love, and so on; but three points concern us here:

- Unity
- Indissolubility
- Open-ness to children

Marriage involves, *inter alia*, these three things; and the deliberate exclusion of one or any of them from the consent given by the parties, means that whatever was called consent was in some way defective; and the marriage may be invalid. Consent whole and entire is required.

The law of the Code first states the presumption that internal consent is presumed to conform to the outward acts and signs used in the celebration of marriage; and 'if, however, either or both parties should by a positive act of will exclude marriage itself', (total simulation) or 'any essential element of marriage or any essential property, such a party contracts invalidly' (can.1101)

Excluding the Right to Conjugal Acts

It must always have seemed strange and lacking in good taste to describe a loving act of intercourse between two validly married persons as an expression of a 'right to the conjugal act'. But this must be seen in its full context. Every human being has rights; the right to life, the right to decide whether to submit to an operation or not, and so on. Human existence carries certain things with it, as it were the expression and exercise of human existence. One of the central properties of marriage is procreation, and within marriage this is a right: the man or woman in the street thinks of marriage as taking with it that fundamental quality, and that it would be a violation of their rights to be deprived of it. This is expressed legally as the right to acts which of themselves are apt for the procreation of children (as well as, of course, their upbringing).

Each person, in marriage, is seen as exchanging with his or her partner these rights over the body: 'what is mine becomes yours; what is yours becomes mine'. The Church, of course, teaches that this exchange is only permitted within marriage; but equally, if this exchange is not made, then it is not marriage. The exchange of these 'rights' between the parties is necessary for marriage; and where the exchange is not made the union is not valid.

What has been expressed above is stated in legal terms. Normally speaking, when two people marry, they do not give a thought to the exchange of these rights. Nonetheless, in another sense, the couple know only too well that this exchange should take place. For example, after the marriage they know something is wrong if it appears that these rights have not been exchanged. Thus, if a woman discovers after the marriage that her husband refuses her the right to have children, she knows instinctively that there is something terribly wrong with the marriage even if, as is likely, she has no knowledge of Canon Law. The law of the Code mentioned above is merely the legal statement of facts which every man and woman knows through their own nature, and through their own natural appreciation of what marriage means.

Having said that the exclusion of the right to conjugal acts would render a marriage null and void, we must now see what is meant more precisely by the exclusion of the right to conjugal acts. There are a number of different situations which are covered by this statement. One situation is where a man for some reason absolutely refuses his wife intercourse. Sometimes this situation does arise, and after a few years the wife, broken in health and spirit, finally admits that her husband never once allowed her to have intercourse. Another situation is where one of the parties insists that intercourse should take place only within the safe period. Never once did he or she permit intercourse to take place at any other time. The third situation is when one of the parties insists upon making use of contraceptives whenever intercourse takes place. This insistence upon contraceptives is quite clearly, and upon the person's own admission, so as to avoid all possibility of allowing the wife to have children. In all three situations – assuming there is clear proof – the union would be invalid because one of the parties refused the right 'to acts which of themselves are suitable for the generation of children'.

What is vital in the examination of any marriage case is that the intention to exclude the right to proper conjugal acts is known to have existed *at the time of the wedding*. It is obvious that an intention formulated *after* the wedding has taken place would not mean that the right had been excluded from consent. Only where the contract is mutilated by some exclusion from the consent at the time of the wedding would the union itself be invalid.

Bearing in mind that a person who enters a union with the clear, firm intention of not transferring to his partner the rights over his own body to conjugal acts would be entering the union with defective consent, it must also be said that a person entering marriage merely with the intention of abusing the rights to such acts *already conferred* would not contract invalidly. It is, possible to think of a situation where a man freely and willingly grants his wife *the right* to conjugal acts, but proposes for some of the time to abuse his rights by insisting on contraceptive intercourse, against her will. In these circumstances, assuming the right has not been excluded from the marital consent, the marriage would be regarded as, at least *prima facie*, valid. For example, if a newly married couple agree to make use of contraceptives until they are able to afford to start a family, they would not contract invalidly. Nor would a marriage be invalid where, contrary to the wife's wishes, the husband makes use of contraceptives on some or most occasions of intercourse.

In these situations, the judges in the case have to try to decide what the intentions of the person were when he entered marriage. As we will see later on, the burden of proof is upon the person alleging the invalidity, and it cannot be presumed that because one of the parties insists on contraceptive intercourse that he has therefore excluded the right to conjugal acts from his consent. This must be proved. To determine the precise intentions of the parties existing at the time of the marriage is obviously extremely difficult, and it is for this reason that a large quantity of evidence often has to be collected.

It is also important to appreciate, when considering an intention to exclude the right to conjugal acts, that this intention must be a *real* one. An intention is a proposal formulated by the will, and not merely the knowledge of something in the intellect. For example, to say: 'I trust and hope we shall not have children' does not constitute an intention, since there is no specific act of the will formulated here. On the other hand, to say: 'I do not propose to have any children' is an indication of an act of will. As such, it would be described as an intention. It could be that one of the parties had never given thought, before the marriage, to the matter of children. Such a person might afterwards say: 'I did not make any act of will excluding children from the marriage, because I did not consider the matter. But if I had considered it, I would have excluded them'. Such a statement would merely mean that in certain circumstances an act of will would have been made, but the phrasing of the statements indicates that an act of will upon this vital matter was in fact not made. This type of intention ('I would have, had I known') is not sufficient to invalidate the marriage.

The exclusion is no way has to be a permanent one. On the one hand a person may intend never to allow his wife the rights to acts of themselves suitable for the procreation of children, and this entirely against her will. That would be a permanent intention. But, on the other hand, this same persons may intend to exclude the right to proper intercourse for a time. In this case the person also contracts invalidly, because the right to these acts exists from the start of the marriage.

The phrase has been used above: 'against his wife's wishes'. It happens more often than not that a young couple decide when they marry to postpone starting a family for a while; for example, until they have their own accommodation. That is to say, they have given each other the right, but they will take steps, such as the infertile period, not to use the right for the time being. Notice, they have both agreed to this. In ordinary circumstances, when they get a house and they have settled down, by mutual agreement they start their family. But what is important about their arrangement is this: they must effectively agree that one of the parties may unilaterally change his or her mind and rescind the agreement. If this were not so, then one party would entirely and absolutely exclude the right to those acts 'of themselves suitable for the pro-creation of children' until they have moved into their house. This would mean that it was no longer just an agreement between both to postpone; but an intention of one of them to exclude, albeit for the time being. This is a point which judges must carefully bear in mind when weighing the evidence in such a case.

Equally, the judges have to be aware that an agreement between the parties to postpone, does not of itself mean an exclusion by both parties. Moreover, mutual agreement between the couple not to have children (either for a time or indeed for ever) does not automatically mean an intention to exclude. This merely spells out what was said earlier about the difference between conveying the right to those acts, but agreeing not to make use of them. There have been many examples of good Christian married couples who for special reasons have agreed not to have children in their union, but in no way acted in any fashion contrary to the Church's teaching on marriage.

The basic point is, that what invalidates on this heading

is an intention to remove the other person's right to those conjugal acts of themselves suitable for the procreation of children. Any such intention, whether for ever, for a time, or even until a person decides it is the right time, invalidates the marriage.

Examples of Exclusion of the Right to Conjugal Acts

Michael and Olivia

*Two graduate students, **Michael** and **Olivia**, married in the Register Office. Olivia was a Catholic. The couple intended to return to their home town and there celebrate the marriage in Olivia's parish church. This did in fact happen, although there was an interval of some ten days between the civil marriage and the wedding in the Church. Even before the civil marriage, Olivia thought she sensed on the part of Michael an unwillingness to discuss the matter of children. But on the honeymoon, after the Church wedding, Michael insisted on using contraceptives, in spite of his wife's protest. The excuse he made was that they could not afford children at the time. However, as time went by, it became clear to Olivia that Michael was never going to have children by her, and not long before they parted he told her so in as many words. In fact it emerged that just before the time of the civil union Michael would have been prepared to have children, but after the civil ceremony Michael happened to speak to some friends who told him that 'Catholics had to have children and lots of them'. He disliked this idea intensely, and before the church wedding he made a clearly formulated intention not to have any children at all by Olivia. He made this intention quite clear to the friends he was speaking with and hence, at the time of the church wedding, he had already formed an intention to exclude the right to proper conjugal acts with his wife. The case was decided in favour of invalidity.*

Cecilia and Anthony

Cecilia was engaged to **Richard**. Previously, Cecilia had become involved in a rather way-out environmental group which preached that having children was a disservice to the environment. Richard did not agree with this at all, and when Cecilia told him that the logical conclusion of these views was that they would not have children in their forthcoming union, he terminated the engagement. Cecilia was very upset because she 'wanted to be married'. So when she became involved with **Anthony**, she did not tell him about these views and the marriage was then celebrated. After the marriage Cecilia made use of the pill and the coil, unknown to Anthony. Meanwhile, he had not been concerned about the non-arrival of children; but then Cecilia decided she did not wish to continue with the pill or the coil and told Anthony to make use of a sheath or to be sterilised. This started a conversation from which it emerged precisely what Cecilia's true ideas were about not having a family. As a result of this the relationship quickly broke down and the couple separated. It did not take Anthony long to discover what Cecilia's true views had been at the time of the previous engagement and at the time of their own marriage. The case was decided in favour of invalidity.

Rupert and Chantel

Rupert was 34 and **Chantel** 24 when they married. Rupert was much (especially in his own eyes) a man of the world and regarded Chantel as a child. On the contrary, Chantel was a very bright, young, newly-qualified accountant and anything but a child. Rupert belonged to a fashionable gaming club; and there was conversation with his friends and fellow gamblers about the forthcoming wedding. His colleagues had remarked on the age difference and wondered whether Rupert was making the right choice, charming and attractive as Chantel was. They also *pointed out that if this marriage turned out to be a mistake, Rupert would be rash to take on family responsibilities. However, Rupert rather loftily informed his friends that he would marry the girl; and whatever her ideas might be, he would decide, depending upon the nature of the relationship and the qualities of Chantel, as to when, or even whether there would be children. The marriage took place; but Rupert insisted that Chantel take the Pill and indeed for some time supervised this daily. Early on Chantel thought this was quite a good idea since it allowed her to settle down and run the apartment as well as to do her professional job. But after two years she thought, especially in view of Rupert's age, that they should be considering starting a family. She put this to Rupert but he told her quite clearly that he had not decided yet whether to have a family at all; and anyway he would tell her when he had decided! Following this conversation, he also made use of contraceptives in case Chantel stopped taking the Pill. Not long after this the marriage broke down when he started an affair. There was clear pre-marriage evidence of his intention to decide 'if and when' there would be children; as well as his admission afterwards; and the circumstantial evidence of his use of contraceptives. The case was decided in favour of nullity.*

Intention to Exclude Indissolubility

Whatever may have been the practice of the Jews until the time of Christ, Jesus clearly stated that what had gone before was not God's meaning of marriage; and the Church understands Christ to have stated with utter clarity that marriage was something permanent, without any concept of divorce about it. This has been the Church's constant teaching through the ages, and this is why the Code following the Second Vatican Council regards indissolubility as one of the essential properties of marriage (cf can.1056). What this effectively involves is that once a person is validly and sacramentally married he or she is always married, regardless of the *de facto* breakdown of the common life.

Practically speaking, therefore, a person who enters into the state of matrimony is considered as having entered into a state that is permanent; and that the bond of marriage will remain whatever happens subsequently. It is quite understandable that for some reason the common life may break down; but the 'bond' which was established by the proper consent of the parties is not thereby revoked by the fact of a couple separating. There is an assumption which arises if a person goes through a recognisable ceremony of marriage that the person intends to enter into a permanent state as established by God. This is, of course, a presumption; and all presumptions cede to proof to the contrary.

It is however possible for a person to enter into a union with the deliberate intention of terminating it in certain circumstances. In such a case, if the details can be established through the evidence, then that union will be declared null and void. What is required is that the person concerned has a specific, clear and formulated intention to exclude the property of indissolubility from marriage. A deliberate act of will in rejecting such a clear essential element of marriage is required for the union to be invalid.

Unlike the previous ground we considered (the intention to exclude the right to conjugal acts) the ground of the exclusion of indissolubility does not allow the possibility to distinguish between the *exclusion* of an obligation and the *non-fulfilment* of that obligation. The permanence of marriage is either excluded or not. Once it is excluded, subject to proof, the marriage is regarded as null and void.

From a practical point of view, this ground of nullity presents a number of problems. To illustrate one problem, if a man were to say to his fiancée that he did not necessarily intend the marriage to be permanent, there is a strong possibility that she would not then marry him at all. More often, the man would not mention his intentions to his fiancée before the marriage. Hence, evidence would have to be found, if at all, amongst the man's friends to whom he may have communicated his pre-marital intentions.

Of course, it must also be remembered that both parties may enter a union in which neither regards it as necessarily permanent; and have communicated this intention to each other. Naturally, the reasons why they so agreed on a mutually rescindable union would have to be closely inspected; but this is certainly a heading for examination by the Church's Courts. It is quite clear that person with an absolute intention to set aside a marriage at some time in the future would contract invalidly. Likewise a person or both parties who reserved to themselves individually or jointly the right to set aside the marriage based upon some event in the future, for example unhappiness or cessation of the common life, equally contracts invalidly based upon an hypothetical exclusion of permanence.

The permanence of the marriage may never even have dawned upon one or both the parties. What they call their 'marriage' is thus completely different from what the Church, its law and most Christians understand it to be. If this were shown by evidence to be the case, then they could hardly be presumed to have entered into the state of Christian marriage. Thus, although it could not specifically be said that the person excluded Christian marriage, it could equally well be said that the the same person did not enter (or intend to enter) a Christian marriage. The Church's jurisprudence has tended to regard this as equivalent to an implicit exclusion of permanency; and depending upon the evidence and the circumstances, decisions in this kind of case have been for nullity. In general, however, this kind of situation is a fairly rare one. In the average situation, what must be established is the clear exclusion of permanence from the marriage consent, and this by clear uniquivocal evidence.

A point of considerable importance here concerns the

existence of civil divorce, and its effect upon a person's thinking, or understanding of marriage. One approach is that of a person who grows up in a place where divorce exists. It cannot be said that such a person is ignorant of the existence of divorce. The tabloid newspapers (indeed some of the broadsheets) are packed with information about who's marriages have broken down; and who is presently escorting who's wife. The *de facto* impermanence of marriage is therefore hardly a well-preserved secret! But as so often happens, this young couple entering their marriage know all about these breakdowns, but the thought of break-down, though they know it occurs, simply does not occur to them as a possibility in their own case.

On the other hand, a person may grow up in a milieu in which divorce is so common in his own family circle, as well as that of his friends, that the concept of permanence in marriage is completely alien to his or her thinking. His upbringing has not been tinged with any Christian affiliation. Marriages do indeed take place, but almost as often they end in divorce and each party remarries; and the second union lasts or does not, according to the circumstances. A demonstration of the effect of such a social ambience is that young persons often do not regard formal marriage as relevant to the situation; and they live together quite happily without the 'benefit of clergy'. When such a relationship breaks down, there may well be economic disadvantages, particularly for the woman, and especially if she has children. Hence, marriage tends to be looked upon as a legal device which ensures that when the relationship breaks down neither party is left at an economic disadvantage.

In the following examples, the stress is upon *hypothetical exclusion*. These are the cases most usually dealt with by the Tribunals, since *absolute exclusion* more often has the aspect of total simulation. The proof of the fact or event before the marriage which triggers this hypothetical exclusion is crucial to the judges' consideration of the case.

Examples of Exclusion of Permanence

Jennifer and Edward

Jennifer *was baptised as a Catholic in infancy. She had a Catholic father (who rarely went to church) and a non-Catholic mother. Jennifer grew up in a not very religious atmosphere and ran wild as a teenage girl. She began going out with a young man,* **Edward***, who was quite the reverse in character. He was also a Catholic, and under his influence Jennifer started to go to Mass again. However, she frequently grew impatient with Edward, probably resenting his kindly, stable and honest disposition. During this time she still had occasional flirtations with other young men and one of these occasions involved her in intimacy. Jennifer became pregnant, and the boy responsible disappeared when he was told. Jennifer turned in desperation to Edward. He suggested he should marry Jennifer. He said he loved her, and he would regard the child as his own. Jennifer refused at first, saying that she would rather have an abortion than marry, since a person could make such a terrible mistake by marrying the wrong person. But rather than tell her mother about the pregnancy, she eventually agreed to marry Edward. She told several of her friends, however, that this was a mere matter of convenience for her, since if Edward did not please her, she would leave him and find another man whom she liked better. Unfortunately, no-one told Edward of this, and though the marriage took place happily enough, it was not long after the birth of the baby that Jennifer began to find Edward's goodness a little too oppressive for her. She deserted him within a year of the marriage, leaving him with the baby.*

Edward, after numerous attempts to persuade Jennifer to return to him, finally acknowledged defeat. Subsequently he petitioned his local Tribunal for a declaration of nullity on the grounds of Jennifer's defective intention concerning the permanence of marriage. After taking evidence of Edward and Jennifer, and then from several of

Jennifer's friends who knew her before the marriage, the union was declared null and void on the grounds of Jennifer's deliberate exclusion of the permanence of marriage. It will be noticed here that Jennifer's intention was an hypothetical one: that is, she did not say to herself before the marriage: 'I will leave Edward and go with another man'; she had said rather: 'If I do not find that I get on with Edward, I will leave him'. This hypothetical intention is sufficient to render the marriage invalid, since it also rejects the inherent indissolubility of marriage from the contract.

Dane and Sharon

Dane *and* **Sharon** *were 20 and 19 respectively when they decided to marry. They had known each other for a couple of years, originally meeting at a Sports Centre. They had not had much education, but were equally keen on sports and well-matched physically. She was a telephonist, and he was a telephone engineer. They got on well together and they had their sporting interests in common. But although their friends regarded them as a well-matched pair, they also thought that they were very immature, at least emotionally. Their friends were very frank with them and there were lots of conversations about the wisdom, or lack of it, in respect of their marrying. However, by this time the couple were engaged in a very active sexual relationship, and it seemed to them that marriage would merely continue this rather pleasant existence. They both realised that their friends might have a point about them being rather too young to marry. Nevertheless – neither were Catholics – they decided they would marry, but because they like each other a lot, they also agreed between them that if anything went wrong with their relationship they would regard each other as quite free again. They even made this clear to their friends. The marriage took place; and within three years the relationship did indeed break down. They divorced, and Edward subsequently* *remarried. Sharon then met a Catholic and wished to marry. A case was put before the local Tribunal, and the evidence was adequate to show that the union was invalid on the grounds of hypothetical exclusion of permanence.*

Intention to Exclude Fidelity

Parallel with the essential property of indissolubility or permanence of marriage, there is the equally essential property of fidelity. If either the unity or fidelity of the marriage is excluded by one of the parties, then the marriage is invalid. When a person contracts marriage he (or she) is presumed to include within the matrimonial consent all that marriage involves. Amongst other things, he is presumed to include the essential property of fidelity within marriage. Of course, more often than not, a person would rarely consider the matter of infidelity. When people marry, Tribunal experience shows, they embrace the property of fidelity wholeheartedly. However, Marriage Tribunals deal with the out-of-the-ordinary situation.

To begin with it needs to be said that many people, if not most, enter marriage with no thought of an exclusion of fidelity. On the other hand, a person who has led a 'full life', while he may well intend to be faithful to his wife, cannot always eliminate a weakness that might lead him into danger, and even into infidelity. This, however, could not be classed as indicating an intention against fidelity.

There are two situations which need to be mentioned here, the first much more rare than the second. There is a certain cultural ethos which regards the existence of a mistress with some equanimity. Indeed, at other times and in other countries, this was not unusual amongst a certain class of person. It was maintained that in order that there should be marital harmony, the husband might discreetly keep a mistress, but in a way such as not to harm the marital life-style or the prosperity of the proper spouse. Indeed it was not unknown that the wife or the husband's mother might select and approve a 'suitable mistress' for the husband! Those days are mostly past; but vestiges of this thinking still persist. This, of course, is a classic example of an intention against fidelity: the intention to operate a sort of *mariage à trois*.

The second situation is more common in the present day. There is a well-defined attitude amongst some persons that sexual liberty is a requirement of the modern age. This is realised in a number of different situations as the cases below will demonstrate. However, the primary element here is that fidelity within marriage is simply not thought of as relevant any more. What faces us here is an explicit rejection of fidelity as an element of marriage, or at least an approach by which fidelity has no specific essential place in marriage. Where a Court is able to conclude that to all intents and purposes fidelity was rejected from this marriage, established of course by adequate and convincing proof, the union in question must be declared null and void.

Examples of Exclusion of Fidelity

Frederick and Yvonne

Frederick and **Yvonne** *were married after a fairly lengthy courtship. Not long before the marriage, Frederick presented Yvonne with a document for both of them to sign. The document appeared to deal with property settlements, and amongst these details was a statement that Frederick intended to have complete freedom and liberty in 'everything'. Yvonne regarded this statement as somewhat cryptic, and she did not understand the full import of the statement until after the marriage. On the honeymoon, Frederick was reproved for his conduct with other women. At once, he declared that Yvonne had granted him complete freedom in this and all other matters, in the document both had signed. From the very beginning of the marriage, Frederick conducted himself as one who appeared to have no intention of binding himself by* *marriage and its obligations. These facts were confirmed by other witnesses, and Frederick himself confirmed under oath that the meaning of the cryptic phrase in the document had been that he was reserving to himself the right to have intercourse with other women. All the evidence demonstrated moreover, that Frederick had conducted himself in this manner since the beginning of the marriage. This was a clear case of the exclusion of the obligation of fidelity in marriage, and the petitioner, Yvonne, was granted a decree of nullity.*

Natalie and Franco

Franco *and* **Natalie** *had had a two-year courtship; but the couple were only able to meet a couple of times a fortnight, due to Franco's work: he was a long-distance lorry driver. In fact, even during the engagement to Natalie, on his days away from home, Franco had a girl friend in each of the centres to which he travelled with his heavy goods lorry. The courtship with Natalie involved a sexual relationship, but there were also relationships with at least three other girls, all equally and fully sexual. Franco did not indicate to any of these girls away from home that he was engaged, and of course he did not tell Natalie about the other relationships. It emerged later that Franco had been careful enough to locate the three other girls as far from each other as possible, as well as far from home where Natalie was.*

The marriage was celebrated and after a two-week honeymoon, Franco resumed his lorry driving and his relationships with the other girls. It came to light later on that he had not told the other girls of his marriage; and it was subsequently discovered that all three of them (single) had been awaiting Franco to propose marriage to them. In fact he was engaged to two of them, when one followed him back to London, suspicious that he was not being faithful to her. This girl, **Amanda,** *discovered that Franco was living in a house with another girl (Natalie) and there* *was an appalling scene. Eventually it all came out and Natalie left Franco, who was most upset and quite bewildered at the breakdown of his marriage and the relationship with Amanda. Evidence subsequently showed that Franco had been quite intent on maintaining these other relationships outside the marriage (relationships which had been started before the engagement to Natalie). It was clearly proved that he had excluded fidelity from his consent in marrying Natalie and a decree of nullity was issued.*

Conditions

Thus far we have been examining the nullity of marriage from the point of view of a person making an absolute, or at least an hypothetical, intention against marriage itself; or against some essential element or property of marriage. That is to say, an intention to 'exclude' something. However, another situation can arise in which a person can give consent that is subject to some kind of condition. A condition can concern the future as well as the past and the present.

It may seem strange in our modern culture that such a point is even relevant. However, it must be clear that marriage has always been very much part of the social and cultural setting. In certain, indeed in nearly all, parts of Western Europe some three or four hundred years ago, many marriages were very much a matter of the union of this family with that one. The union involved very considerable and careful negotiations with regard to family, dynasty, property, rights, wealth, and the like. In fact it was far too important to leave to be determined merely by the 'love' of a couple, one for another. Marriages were typically 'arranged', so that the best results might come from them. Of course, this did not preclude a couple from wholeheartedly supporting the decision of their parents but such support was very much an adjunct, and the resulting union (always assuming that it was not entered into by reason of force and fear) would be quite valid.

It is only in the last two to three hundred years (and in many places much less) that marriage has been 'privatised' as it were, the union depending upon the decision of the couple themselves, hopefully with the parents' consent. But in the light of what happened in the past, it will be appreciated that the arrangements for a marriage could be very complicated when consideration was to be given to such matters as property, inheritance, titles and land. Since these were very much contractual elements, it can also be seen that terms and conditions could play a vital part in such negotiations. Hence the law of the Church had to reflect what was happening socially and culturally, and had its formal canonical views on the legitimacy of conditions attached to marriage arrangements and indeed of the validity of marriages which may have been entered into, subject to various conditions. It is for this reason that the Code of Canon Law has to deal with such conditions.

It should also be mentioned that the law of the Church was to some extent different under the 1917 Code to that in force since the 1983 Code. But although this sounds as if there are different laws for people married before 1983 and those married since, the situation is in fact really quite straightforward.

The best way to approach the matter is to distinguish between two major kinds of conditions. The first kind concerns conditions relating to the past or to the present. 'I will marry you if it is true that you were never formally engaged to Sonia' (he either was engaged to Sonia or he was not). 'I will marry you if you are are a virgin' (she either is a virgin or she is not). If a person entered marriage and he or she applied such a condition to the consent, the consent given will be effective depending upon whether the past or the present condition is fulfilled. If he actually *was* engaged to Sonia, or she is not a virgin then the consent by the partner has *de facto* no effect. And since it is consent which brings marriages into being, the marriage is null and void. The law of the Code says: 'Marriage entered into subject to a condition concerning the past or the present is valid or not according to whether the condition exists or not. (can.1102,§2)

However, there is another kind of condition, which concerns the future: 'I marry you on condition that the children will be baptised as Catholic'. One can imme diately see the problem here. Until the children (and there may be none) are born of the union, is the consent suspended or not? If there are children and all but the last one are baptised, is the consent suspended or not? If it was suspended, when is the consent regarded as having effectively been given? This area was a complete jungle under the old Code. Various kinds of future conditions were distinguished, for example future necessary conditions, or future moral conditions, or future impossible conditions. The legal and jurisprudential difficulties of all these will immediately be perceived.

The new law has simplified matters very considerably by stating quite bluntly that any marriage contracted subject to a future condition is invalid. (can.1102,§1) Moreover, although this is the law of the new Code, this law is regarded as governing marriages which took place under the old law. Thus a marriage which took place before 1983 subject to a condition concerning the future would be regarded as invalid.

Clearly proof of such conditions, whether future, past or present, is vital. This proof may not be difficult to obtain if there are documents or attestable verbal agreements. But all Marriage Tribunals are well aware of the possibility of self-deception in this particular area. it is not difficult, after the breakdown of a marriage, for a person to think 'had I know this or that fact I would never have married her'. This itself can be completely unmalicious and understandable self-deception; and this can also very easily be turned into a 'condition': 'If I had known that she had been promiscuous before I met her, I would not have married her. I made it a condition of marriage that she had never been promiscuous'. Hence, clear and uncontestable evidence must be put forward before the judges can regard the allegation of a condition as established.

Finally, if a priest is helping to arrange a marriage and discovers that a condition concerning the future has been made, he is obliged to tell the couple that as long as the condition remains, they may not marry. Not only must the priest refuse to celebrate the marriage, the law completely forbids it. The only course for the priest is to have the couple, or whichever party had made the future condition, to rescind it. Moreover, because of the circumstances, he would require solid evidence that it has indeed been rescinded, for example by means of a sworn document attesting to the removal of the condition.

There is also a stricture about conditions concerning the past and the present. Such a condition may not lawfully be attached to the consent without the express, written, permission of the Bishop. It is not sufficient for the celebrating priest to allow it; the whole matter must be referred to the Bishop for his adjudication. The pastoral implications of both these provisions are quite clear.

Chapter Four

CONSENT AFFECTED BY EXTERNAL FACTORS

SO FAR, we have been speaking about consent to marriage which has been deliberately and entirely withheld or consent which has been mutilated so that part of the object of that consent has been deliberately excluded.

Forced Consent

We now come to a ground for nullity where, by implication, consent was actually given; but that consent was in some sense constrained or produced by fear. We are not here talking solely about physical force. Certainly, if one could actually imagine it, an act which is caused by physical force would be regarded by the Code as invalid. (can.125,§1) For example, an elderly and infirm person's hand is physically forced to sign a document, for example a will. But such circumstances of pure physical force are, of course, hardly likely to arise in connection with marriage. Of course, if such circumstances should actually occur, then the matter would be dealt with quite separately, under a different heading, namely, where the person has no use of human reason at all. There is no human act. (see page 88, *Amentia*). But what can exist prior to marriage is a kind of force, moral force, which itself induces fear.

Marriage is an intimate and lifelong community of conjugal love,which involves the freedom dignity and fulfilment of two people. It brings with it onerous obligations. Obviously this kind of commitment demands total freedom. Moreover, the law is not merely talking about marriage between Christians. The dignity of marriage can exist in a non-sacramental form among those who are not Christians, and the need for freedom of consent applies to all marriages whether Christian or non-Christian. That is to say, this freedom is a requirement of the natural law.

The law of the Code says that a marriage is invalid if it is entered into by a reason of force or grave fear imposed from outside, even if not purposely, and from which the person has no escape other than by choosing marriage. (can.1103) It will be noted that the words 'force' and 'fear' go together. It is quite possible to conceive of a situation in which a person experiences a fear which is really quite irrational or at least is caused by internal thoughts or conflicts. One person may be afraid that his shares are going to drop in price; a girl petrified with embarrassment at the thought of meeting a certain young man in the street; another person may be terrified that he has left the gas on when he left the house. All these are internal fears, and engendered by internal forces or pressure. It will also be quite clear that all these fears are to a greater or lesser extent subjective and unreasoned.

On the other hand, there are fears which are engendered by an outside source, namely by reason of 'force', but of the moral kind. Moral force is regarded seriously: it is the fear born of moral force that will invalidate a marriage. What is meant by 'force' in the context of marriage? Force involves something which exerts pressure on the person's will by means of the threat of some evil, so that the will, which otherwise would not have done so, chooses marriage to escape from that evil. This, as already stated, does not concern the kind of inner compulsion caused by psychiatric or psychological disorders. (see page 92, *Lack of Due Discretion*). It is also important to stress that there must be the threat or at least the perception of such threat, of some harm or evil. The person is not left without a choice, but the choice is between marriage on the one hand, and the evil or harm perceived on the other hand. There is stress on the term 'perceived'; because the person could quite wrongly perceive the evil or harm which indeed may not exist at all. It could be, for example, that the perceived threat of bodily harm or a moral pressure arises from the threat of imprisonment or loss of employment. In each case the perception could be quite wrong; i.e. there is in fact no real threat of bodily harm, or of imprisonment or of loss of employment. But essentially it is the person's perception that is here involved.

Fear from an External Agent

The Oxford Dictionary describes fear as *Painful emotion caused by impending danger or evil;* the 'painful emotion' is really better termed trepidation. Of its nature fear is a subjectively internal phenomenon; and in the context of the law which we are examining (can.1103) this fear is a trepidation resulting from force. Underlying the whole of the jurisprudence in connection with force and fear is the fundamental injustice in denying the person true freedom of choice. Injustice, of course, can only be caused by a free agent; that is why fear caused by intrinsic factors (psychiatric or psychological disorders) does not come within the scope of the present ground. The distinction between fear caused by internal or external factors can be shown by means of an example. A teenage, unmarried girl becomes pregnant. Teenage pregnancies in some societies can produce a high level of fear and anxiety. This might involve the fear of loss of reputation, the fear of eternal punishment, embarrassment; all these elements are, of course, intrinsic and would not render the marriage (should it have taken place) null and void. On the other hand, this same girl, on revealing the fact of the pregnancy to her parents, could become so intimidated by them that she was left with no practical alternative other than getting married; this fear would be extrinsic and therefore invalidating. It will, therefore, be seen that the first requirement to establish the ground of force and fear is that the fear is caused by an extrinsic or external source.

Grave Fear

The second requirement to establish this ground is that fear must be grave. What is grave fear? The answer is, of course, that it can vary depending upon the person and the circumstances. Thus, a really serious and very grave fear for one person might be no more than a passing worry or anxiety for another. Objective, or absolute, grave fear would affect everyone, not just this or that kind of person.

For example, this might involve the fear of death, serious bodily harm or even mutilation. No-one could regard any of those as a passing worry or mere anxiety: on the other hand, a much lesser degree of fear existing in another person might have, to all intents and purposes, exactly the same results as objective grave fear. This lesser fear, which may be equally paralysing for some persons, is called subjective (or relative) grave fear. Not everyone would regard the fear as serious; a strong-minded person certainly would not. But for this particular person, perhaps because of his or her youth or predisposition, it might be regarded as the threat of a very serious harm or evil. Both these forms of fear, provided the end result is grave, would involve nullity. Obviously, the gravity of the fear and the condition, temperament and character of the person concerned must all be carefully studied. For example, a young girl who has led a very sheltered life, who has always lived at home and who has a soft and pliant disposition, would be far more vulnerable to moral pressure placed upon her by her parents than would a girl a few years older, who has lived away from home in her own flat for some time. Again a girl would probably, though by no means always, be more prone to the effects of moral pressure than a man.

One indication of the gravity of the fear is to see

whether the person concerned took any steps, however ineffectual, to liberate herself from the moral pressure exerted. For example: a girl has been told that her grandparents are especially insistent upon her marrying a particular young man. Her parents do not insist, and an appeal to them would be certain to remove the pressure upon the girl. However, if the girl went to stay with her grandparents in an isolated location in the country, where she might expect to be subjected to serious pressure to marry the young man, she can hardly be described as taking 'reasonable steps' to free herself from the pressure exerted by her grandparents!

A particular area, common in cases of force and fear, concerns the influence of parents (or maybe even of the wider family) upon the situation, and therefore upon the person. This is often called *reverential fear*. This is the kind of situation when a person fears the indignation of a parent or superior, or guardian, even though there may be no blows or threats. This kind of fear of does indeed appear very slight, but if in fact it amounts, for this particular person, to *relatively grave fear*, and leaves the person no liberty of choice but to marry, then it would indeed invalidate the marriage in question. This type of fear will become grave, depending upon the circumstances which surround it. Such circumstances would arise where there is constant nagging, endless harping on the subject, entreaties and similar indirect, but nonetheless very effective assaults on the person to such a degree that she is finally worn down and all resistance is overcome. On the other hand, the mere fear of offending a parent of guardian alone would not amount to *grave reverential fear*; nor, of course, would it be grave reverential fear if a girl married a man who was the preference of her parents, rather than her own preference, provided always that the choice she did make was not against her will. It is to be expected, of course, that a parent will have, and will express strong views on such an important matter.

Marriage the only course possible

When a person experiences fear derived from some external force, two separate situations can be envisaged. One situation is that there is clear *constraint* (force producing fear) upon the person to marry. The only alternatives are either some perceived grave result which would be harmful in the extreme, or marriage. In this case, the force producing the fear was specifically engineered to effect the marriage. The other situation is where there is an external force exerted by her parents (producing internal grave fear) upon a young girl to do something (for example, enter a convent) which is hateful in the extreme to her. The pressure from the parents is relentless and the girl has no possibility of escaping their influence. Eventually, the girl considers that marriage to the only young man that she knows, but whom she heartily despises, will be the lesser of two evils; and she marries to escape the threat.

Both these two situations involve invalidating grave fear. But it will be noticed in the second example that the force inducing the fear was not directly aimed at marriage. But marriage was the sole escape for this girl, and in both cases marriage was the only course possible. It should be noted here that although the terms of the 1917 Code did not include this element, all nullity cases (that is to say which took place before and after the 1983 Code) would be judged according to these norms.

A clause in the present Code underlines yet another point. The law speaks of force or grave fear imposed from outside, even if not purposefully . . . imposed (can.1103). This means that it is not necessary that the person who imposes the force *intends* to inspire fear in the victim. Hence it does not need to be proved that the agent of the fear knew what the possible result of his conduct might be. It is sufficient to show that he did actually inspire the fear, and no more. Moreover, even if the agent does inspire the fear which ends in marriage to a particular person, it is not necessary to prove that he intended the victim to marry that particular person. It is quite sufficient that the victim acted in fear to remove himself or herself from the perceived harm.

Unjustly Imposed Fear

It will be recalled that the quotation from the Code of Canon Law earlier made no reference to the fear having been unjustly incurred. This was a term used in the 1917 Code; the development of jurisprudence between the two Codes saw the removal of the notion of 'unjust' from the ground. The point involved was that any fear produced by an external free agent which resulted in the victim having to choose marriage, over the years came to be regarded as unjust in the context of marriage. The older distinction between just and unjust fear (which no longer exists in the law) derived from a time when parental rights over children were such as to permit parents to direct their offspring towards different actions; but, of course, when this included marriage, the jurisprudence of the Church formed a view on the whole concept of justice and personal rights. Hence, the distinction no longer has a place under this heading of nullity.

Proof of Grave Fear

It goes without saying that the detailed circumstances which lay behind the impugned marriage have to be proved to the extent to moral certainty. Thus, there must be evidence of the gravity (whether objective or subjective) of the external source and of the fact that the person was unable to escape from the harm, or the marriage, which threatened. These are, of course, direct means of proof. An indirect or circumstantial element of proof is termed *aversion*.

Aversion is not lack of love or a lack of attraction towards the person to be married; nor is it reluctance to marry; nor is it repugnance in the person for the person who is to be married. Any of these would be useful. But it is quite sufficient for the person to be averse – not to be proposed partner himself – but *averse to marriage*. Moreover, the aversion must be shown to be existent at the time of the marriage. When there are clear signs that aversion existed before the marriage as well as afterwards, that would indicate aversion existing at the time the consent was given in the ceremony. Finally, not only must the aversion be present at the time of the marriage, but so must the fear; that is to say, it is not enough for there to have been fear during the early days before the marriage; the fear must be shown to have remained up until the time of the marriage.

Examples of Force and Fear

Jack and Cynthia

*Jack was 18 and **Cynthia** was 17 when they met. neither were religious people, and after comparatively brief association the couple began having frequent intimate relations. Not long afterwards Cynthia became pregnant. The girl tried several 'old wives' methods of inducing an abortion, but without success. Eventually Cynthia told Jack that he would have to marry her. At first he refused, and so Cynthia's mother told the boy's mother of the pregnancy. The boy' mother insisted that Jack should marry the girl and this insistence was repeated with constant nagging and anger, together with the threat of turning Jack out of doors if he would not go through with the marriage. Eventually, Jack gave in to this coercion, but even at the last moment he tried to escape by going away with some friends on the night before the marriage. His mother discovered the plan and forbade him to leave the house, and again he capitulated. On the day of the marriage in the Register Office, he brought himself to a state verging on intoxication. The marriage broke down soon afterwards. The marriage was judged to be invalid on the grounds of force and fear.*

It is important to appreciate that the fear which drove Jack to capitulate to his mother's wish did not amount to *terror*. Fear is a much lesser state than this, and it would not be proper for a court to demand as much as this to prove the alleged grounds.

It will also be noted from the above case that the victim of the force was a man. Although from the nature of things it is more frequent that a girl should be the victim of the force suffered at the hands of her parents or guardian, the situation can also arise with a man. However such cases, involving both men and women as petitioners, are not unusual.

Penelope and Roger

Roger *was an outstanding veterinary surgeon who had qualified well. Soon afterwards he had been offered a partnership in a particular fashionable veterinary practice which specialised in the care and treatment of racehorses. He was friendly with, but not romantically attached to, the very attractive **Penelope**, daughter of the senior partner of the practice. The girl had attended a very expensive Public School, and went on after that to finishing school in Switzerland. Although friendly with Penelope, Roger was in fact discreetly going out with **Candida**. However, at a party both Roger and Penelope had too much to drink, and they had retired to one of the bedrooms and were caught* in flagrante delicto. *This news was passed on to Penelope's father. He exploded; and told Roger that since this episode was known about he would have to marry Penelope. If he did not, the father would dismiss him and pass Roger's name around the racing and veterinary fraternity; and this would in practise preclude him from ever getting a comparable job. Roger succumbed to this pressure, but when the marriage broke down the force and fear that had been applied was sufficient to produce a decree of nullity.*

Charmian and Alan

Charmian aged 24 and her younger brother **Alan** aged 16 were the children of an extremely wealthy stockbroker. The two young persons were kidnapped by a particulary vicious gang with anarchist tendencies. An enormous sum was sought by way of ransom for the two. The treatment they received was appalling and needlessly violent. The negotiations between a security firm employed by the father and the kidnappers were prolonged and frustration grew. It seemed to Charmian and to Alan that as the delay lengthened their treatment grew worse. Eventually, to speed up the negotiations the kidnappers sliced off Alan's thumb and sent it to the father, indicating they would repeat this course every three days. Charmian was nearly beside herself; but she decided that she would make a set at the leader of the kidnappers; and actually persuaded him that she would marry him if they would harm the couple no further.The group secretly went to Wales; civil notice was given under assumed names; and the couple were married in the Register Office. The ransom was paid; the group was still undetected; and they set off to return to the Middle East. At this stage, with vigilance relaxed, Charmian and Alan escaped. A decree of nullity was eventually granted, principally based on the evidence of Alan; and the intelligent observation of one of the witnesses at the Register Office ceremony.

It will be seen that in the first case there was clear force and fear, probably of a reverential kind. In the second, the real harm which threatened Roger was not only a passing damage to his career, but probably the danger of never being able to work as a vet with racehorses again (the loss of a very lucrative profession). In the third case, the force which produced the fear had nothing to do with marriage; marriage was chosen as a course to prevent further violence and maybe loss of life. In this case the judges did have some very serious and prolonged discussion as to whether the grounds ought not to be total simulation: however they settled for force and fear, as shown

Ignorance of the Nature of Marriage

In order to enter the state of marriage, it is obviously necessary that the person should not be ignorant of what the phrase 'state of marriage' implies. The law of the Code indicates the basic minimum knowledge; although interestingly the Code expresses this in a negative rather than a positive fashion: 'for matrimonial consent to exist, it is necessary that the contracting party is not ignorant of . . .' Putting the matter that way round then accords with a further statement about such ignorance (after puberty) not being presumed.

The basic three elements of which a contracting party must not be ignorant are:

- Marriage is a permanent partnership between a man and a woman.
- It is ordered to the procreation of children.
- There should be some form of sexual co-operation (cf can.1096,§1)

It has already been seen that one of the essential elements of marriage is its permanence. Indeed the wilful exclusion of permanence invalidates marriage. But if exclusion of permanence invalidates, ignorance of permanence equally invalidates. Moreover, this permanent partnership is between a man and a woman (in the singular) which means it is exclusive to these two and not shared with any others. Then since the whole of marriage is geared among other ends to the procreation of children even if this does not always eventuate, ignorance of this element would equally mean a defective consent. The procreation of children must be known to be by way of some form of sexual or bodily co-operation. It is not the jurisprudence of the Church that either partner should have an explicit knowledge of the mechanics of intercourse: it suffices that there is some knowledge that bodily co-operation is necessary.

It is unusual in the present day for there to be cases of ignorance in general, particulary of the sexual aspect, but it is always possible for a person to have literally no knowledge whatsoever of the permanence of marriage. Of course, a person cannot do the impossible. He cannot enter into what is *de facto* a permanent marriage with no concept of permanence at all. But it is equally true that a person who knows that divorce exists obviously also knows that there are many cases where it does not occur. Hence, to such a person more often than not the concept of divorce takes with it a concept of permanence where divorce is not applied. Therefore it is rarely that ignorance is alleged but when it is, then it usually lies in the sexual sphere rather than in any other. In such cases, it is not unheard-of that a union has not been consummated for the very reason of ignorance. The special circumstances of converting a nullity case based on ignorance into a non-consummation case will be dealt with later.

Ignorance: Rosella and Malcolm

Rosella *was a young innocent girl of 18 when she met a sailor named* **Malcolm***. She had had a very protected upbringing; the facts of life had never so much as been mentioned in her home. Courtship with Malcolm involved the constant presence of a chaperone. Prior to the marriage her mother did get as far as mentioning that within the confines of the bedroom, Malcolm might 'do things to her which were somewhat personal' but that she should not mind this, 'that's what men do'. Completely mystified, Rosella went thus into marriage and her honeymoon . She appreciated after the first night what her mother must have been talking about; but she accepted in good part the intimacy which did take place; although had no idea of the connection between this intimacy and children. She was extremely keen on having a family, but thought that* *children would come about through her sleeping between the sheets which Malcolm had slept between. He was a sailor and spent regular fortnightly spells at sea; and on such occasions Rosella solemnly took out the sheets used previously by Malcolm and slept between them in the hope of conceiving a child. The connection between physical intercourse and having a child never occurred to Rosella. In due time she began to complain of the physical intimacy to which she felt she was being subjected by her husband, and not long afterwards returned to her mother. Malcolm alleged Rosella's ignorance was a ground for nullity and when these facts were established and proved, a decree of nullity was granted.*

Error of Person or Quality

The term *error* in Canon Law has a very precise meaning, as one would expect, since there are any number of uses to which we put the word in ordinary conversation. There can be an error in the accounts, an error in spelling. We speak of somebody repenting of the error of his ways, and so on. Error is defined in Canon Law as the false judgement of an object. Quite clearly it is something very different from ignorance. Ignorance is the lack of knowledge, whereas error is a positive judgement which is mistaken. Ignorance exists solely in the intellect, whereas error implies a mistake involved with the function of the will. There are two forms of error, practically speaking, with which the Code of Canon Law, in connection with marriage, is concerned. One is *error of person*, in which a man marries the wrong person, The other is an *error* of quality of a person, but which itself amounts to an error of the person.

Error of a person is quite straightforward. Where a person alleges this type of ground of nullity, also called substantial error, he is actually alleging that the person intended to marry was not the person he did in fact marry. There have been such cases presented before local

Courts and before the Rota, and they make incredible reading. Since in the current law of the Church proxy marriages are still allowed, such cases can arise even today.

Error of Person: Sandro and Caterina

Sandro and **Caterina** met in the south of Italy when they were both 24 and 22 years old respectively. A friendship grew up between them, and after a year or so they thought they would like to get married. However, Sandro did not have a good job, and they both thought that he might improve himself if he went to England and work on the fruit farms there. So Sandro travelled to England and began to work, and after a further year he had saved a substantial sum of money and could certainly afford to marry and keep his wife. In the meanwhile, Caterina had met another young man, **Pietro**, who had much better financial prospects than Sandro. Little by little she realised that she would be happier with Pietro than she would with her own fiancé. She told her parents about her problem, who at first thought that she should marry Sandro, but they too became converted by the realisation that Pietro had better employment and a much brighter future.

Meanwhile Sandro was making arrangements to marry but in England, he wrongly thought that he could not get permission for Caterina to enter the country. However, she would be permitted to enter the country if they were married. Therefore he made use of the device in Canon Law known as Proxy Marriage. By this, he found he had to appoint someone in his home town in Italy to represent him at the marriage ceremony to be celebrated there. He was advised that his representative would make the promises at the altar together with Caterina, at the end of which Sandro would be regarded as married to Caterina. Sandro appointed his future brother-in-law **Giuseppe** as his proxy, and the necessary documents were signed to his effect. The local priest was approached by Caterina's

*parents with the necessary papers, and he agreed to cele-
brate the marriage on a particular Saturday.*

*When the day of the wedding came, Caterina was
adamant that she would not marry Sandro. But in the
meanwhile, her parents has a serious dispute with
Sandro's parents, as a result of which they refused to go to
the church. Taking this opportunity, Caterina sent her
sister **Maria** to the church, and throughout the ceremony,
Maria made the responses together with Sandro's proxy,
Giuseppe. After the wedding ceremony, nobody noticed
anything strange about the young wife keeping her veil
down over her face, and Maria even signed the register in
her own name without anyone noticing.*

*Following the ceremony, Sandro was expecting his wife
to come to England, but she did not arrive on the date
arranged. He made enquiries in Italy and found that
Caterina had indeed left the country, but gone to Argenti-
na with Pietro. When enquiries were made into the matter,
it was discovered that the person who actually had taken
part in the marriage ceremony was Maria and not
Caterina. Therefore the marriage was declared null and
void on the grounds of error of person. It is clear that normally it would only be in a case of a proxy marriage
that such a mix-up could occur so as to amount to the
invalidity of marriage.*

The Code, having dealt with the situation of marrying
the wrong person (can.1097,§1), then goes on to speak of
error about a quality of a person. The law of the Code
says that an error about a quality of a person, even
thought it be the reason for the contract, does not render a
marriage invalid unless that quality was directly and
principally intended (cf can.1097,§2) even if that quality
was the motive for the marriage. For example: a girl has a
number of admirers, but the one whose company she really enjoys is one who makes her laugh. As a result, she
falls in love with him and marries. But it turns out that his
so called humour was a sham. Just because an amusing

companion was her choice and the fact that he appeared to be amusing drew her towards him, and maybe motivated her into marrying him, this would not be sufficient to invalidate the union when she realised he was not the humourous person she had supposed him to be.

This ground concerns the various kinds of quality which may exist. There are certain kinds of quality that are of such significance as to specify or differentiate that person; and the lack of such a quality because it is so significant, might make the person effectively an entirely different person. This is the area of an error of quality which amounts to an error of person. In the older text books the examples given were largely drawn from the dynastic concept of marriage. For example, it was stated that a girl might accept a young man's proposal of marriage thinking wrongly that he was the Prince of Wales; that is , the first son of the monarch and the heir to the throne. However, if he turned out to be the second son, then he would not be the heir to the throne. The older text-books would have regarded the possession of the quality of 'being the Prince of Wales' as of such substance as to make the young man when she actually married him (the second son) a totally different person. But this kind of example of a quality very much concerns an historical age when marriage was considered largely in the dynastic sense. Now, however, there has been a change so that (especially following *Gaudium et Spes*) marriage is considered principally in a personalist sense. It is obvious that this change is also reflected in what might be considered to be the qualities of a person.

Hence, various personal qualities may be considered. Essentially, in accordance with the Code and the Church's jurisprudence, whatever the quality alleged (about which the person was in error), it is necessary that this quality was *directly and principally* intended by the person marrying. This is not to say that a *condition* about the quality was formulated; but it must be established that this quality was in the forefront of the person's mind when marrying.

For example, a girl (indeed probably most girls) would regard herself has having a relationship of trust with her fiancé. She would, in the absence of information to the contrary, regard this relationship and the eventual married relationship as unique to themselves. But say she enters into marriage with a man who had in fact been married before, perhaps in a Register Office and therefore canonically free to marry, and she was quite unaware of this. She was also unaware that the man had children by his first spouse; and that was in the habit of seeing that spouse and the children secretly.

When the girl discovers this, the test would be whether this kind of past and present relationship situation was inimical to the bride's intentions at marriage. If it could be established that her husband's status as unmarried and free of all previous relationships was directly and primarily intended, then there would be grounds of error of quality amounting to an error of person.

Error of quality: Pierre and Odile

Pierre, *a catholic aged 25 entered a civil union in 1938 in France; two children were born of the union. Within a couple of years, he had abandoned his wife and children. He lived initially a life of crime and eventually worked as an informer for the Gestapo in France. He disappeared at the end of the war, but his reputation was such that he was charged and tried in his absence as a collaborator; and was sentenced to thirty years' hard labour. In 1955 he reappeared with a assumed name, altered appearance and bogus credentials. He became engaged to **Odile**, who was 32, and the daughter of a distinguished doctor, a hero of the French Resistance and much respected for his loyalty and bravery during the war, as well as having been decorated personally by General de Gaulle. Pierre, posing as a doctor with a distinguished war record, was much fêted by Odile's family and friends, and the wedding was a celebration of French patriotism. It was only a year or so after the* *wedding that the full truth emerged about Pierre; and he was eventually arrested and sent to prison to serve his sentence. It was quite clear that Odile's primary intention in marrying Pierre was to marry someone like her father with all his special and outstanding characteristics. The contrary qualities in Pierre convinced the judges that there was here an error of quality amounting to an error of person. The real Pierre was a totally different person from the one Odile thought she had married.*

It will be appreciated here that jurists might well discuss whether this case should have been dealt with on the basis of a condition on the part of Odile; or even deceit or fraud exercised by Pierre. But since the case was decided before the new Code of 1983, the ground of error of quality was regarded as entirely appropriate, as well as being completely proved.

Deceit

This particular ground for nullity has had an interesting canonical history. It may come as a surprise to learn that 'deceit' was not mentioned as a ground for nullity in the 1917 Code. It was considered that whatever the reason (leaving aside force and fear) why an innocent, though duped, party entered into marriage, the fact was that that person, regardless of the deceit practiced, had *de facto* given consent. Therefore, the argument went, since proper consent had been given, the marriage was not invalid.

Not every canonist argued this way; and indeed not very long after the publication of the first Code, voices were heard saying that this was clearly wrong and that deceit should be regarded as a ground for nullity; this was specially so in the 1950s and the early 1960s when the documents for the Second Vatican Council were being prepared. But since such topics were not formally discussed at the Council, it was left for development within the Commission for the Revision of the Code. Eventually, the new Code produced the clear statement that a person who enters marriage inveigled by deceit perpetrated in order to secure consent, concerning some quality of the other party, which of its very nature can seriously disrupt the partnership of conjugal life (cf can.1098) contracts invalidly.

It should also be stated that so serious and fundamental do canonists regard the destructive nature of such deceit, that they class it as something which must always have affected the validity of marriage. It is something which must be part of the natural law, not merely some disposition of the positive law of the Church. For this reason, it is held that even marriages which took place before the publication of the new Code would be judged in accordance with the present principle.

The Code attaches a number of qualifications to the law on deceit. The first of these indicates that the person was *inveigled by deceit*. The cause of nullity is deceitful behaviour of some kind which actually results in someone being 'taken in'. Hence, the intention of the agent to deceive would not in itself be sufficient. There must have been an actual and effective deceit. Such deceit can be seen as positive or negative: something may be done to deceive the other party (positive), or something omitted or left unsaid (negative). It does not matter whether the deceit practised was either positive or negative; it suffices that there was deceit, however caused.

Then again, one tends to think of a deceiver and of the person deceived as the two parties to the marriage. This is not necessarily the case. For example, the one deceived may have been taken in by a third party, such as a prospective mother-in-law, or a friend. The identity of the deceiver is not important; what is essential is that there was deceit and one of the parties was deceived, and that without the deception the victim would not have married.

This leads to the second qualification in the law, namely, that the deceit must have been perpetrated so as to secure the consent of the other party, that is to say, the victim would not have married but for the deception.

Thus the motivation of the agent of the deception is important. So, for example, if some deceit was practiced on a victim with some *other* motive than securing his or her consent (and marriage follows), this would not be sufficient to establish the present ground.

It will be seen that this is quite different to the law and the jurisprudence on force and fear, considered above. Under that ground it was not relevant whether the force (leading to the fear) was exercised so as to obtain consent to marriage; it was sufficient that *because* of the force and fear, the person *chose* marriage. However, in the case of deception, the motive for practising the deception must have been specifically geared to produce the person's consent to marriage.

The third qualification concerns some *quality of the other person*, that is, the person whom the victim is deceived into marrying. It has already been said that the deceiver could even be a third party. Hence, the 'other person' is not specifically identified as the agent of the deception; the 'other person' is the other party to the marriage. The quality referred to can be a physical or moral quality.

Then again this quality must be something which of its very nature can seriously disrupt the marital partnership. The terms of the law are extremely important here. It will be seen that the law says it can seriously disrupt the married life; not that it has disrupted it. That means that actual disruption is not necessary, merely that disruption could have happened. For example, it may well be that the victim never ever knew of the deception practised on him or her until after the breakdown of the marriage, which may have happened for quite other reasons.

Of course, this point in the law does leave a great deal open to the subjective element in marriage. This must be so because one is dealing here with what different persons perceive; and perceived reality may well have little to do with objective reality. But this is something which must be left to the judges in an individual case; and they have to take into account the specific circumstances of the marriage as well as the character and the personality of the victim. But there is one element which can guide the judges in this particular matter; that is that the disruption, actual or possible, must be serious. Examples of what could disrupt marital life might be a pregnancy (caused by someone other than the victim); the non-disclosure of AIDS or some other contagious illness; or a criminal record, or even a secret on-going criminal career. It is not difficult to see how these could disrupt marital life, in their various ways.

Deceit: Wanda and Stephen

Wanda is a 30 year-old girl, of much sophistication, with a knowledge of the world, who has become hardened to the life of commerce, in which she holds a senior post. She had a relationship with Stephen which lasted some three years; and it ended when by mischance Wanda discovered that she was pregnant. Her relationship with Stephen had been reasonably discreet; but Stephen was hardly an ornament on the social scene and had been in and out of prison, principally for fraud. When the pregnancy was discovered, Stephen wanted none of it, and departed. Wanda needed to do something quickly. She did not want to have an abortion because if news of that ever became public, her reputation would be irreparably damaged. (She was a publisher of religious books.) She met and pursued Fergus, a serious-minded young man of 27. Fergus was captivated by Wanda; and she had soon enticed him into her bed and intercourse took place. After an appropriate delay, she announced to Fergus that she was pregnant. Believing himself to be the father, he suggested marriage. Wanda 'reluctantly' agreed; and the marriage took place. Initially, for about a year or so it was reasonably happy although Wanda had a miscarriage; but then Wanda tired of the studious and staid Fergus; arguments ensued and Wanda walked out flinging over her shoulder the statement that Fergus had not been responsible for the pregnancy anyway. This marriage was also proved to be null and void on the grounds of deception on the part of Wanda.

It is worth repeating here that all the examples given in this book to illustrate the various possible grounds for nullity are based on real cases, which have been dealt with by Tribunals in the English-speaking world. However, in every case details, places and dates have been changed: and the names are fictional, for obvious reasons.

Chapter Five

PSYCHOLOGICAL GROUNDS

I N CONSIDERING grounds for the annulment of marriage, we have looked at whether consent was given or not; and at what kind of consent was given (full consent, or consent mutilated in some fashion); and certain outside influences that can affect consent. We now examine the person's *power* to give their consent and in what manner this can be affected by internal influences.

There are three areas in which consent can be affected internally, namely *amentia, lack of due discretion* and the *inability to assume the obligations of marriage*. All of these are governed by one canon of the Code (a new one) can.1095. The first part of this canon states that a person who is lacking the use of reason cannot contract validly (can. 1095 n.1). This involves the complicated area of mental disorder. It is an area where the assistance of other sciences, especially in the psychiatric and psychological fields, is vital. This area is made even more difficult because evidence that pre-dates the marriage can be difficult to find. In spite of considerable advances in awareness concerning mental health and sickness, the general public still has a poor understanding of this kind of illness. Indeed, it is true that people may talk more easily these days about cancer than they do about mental disorders. Consequently, evidence is often difficult to obtain.

Sometimes these difficulties can be overcome. Often witnesses have the actual evidence at their fingertips, but are quite unable to see the significance of their knowledge. Skilled evidence taking may well elicit an array of pointers. It is for the judges to try to put these together into a coherent picture, thereby concluding with an affirmative decision.

Amentia

The Latin term has been retained to describe this condition, simply because most translations are either inept, inelegant, or inaccurate. Amentia, for example, does not mean insanity as such, although a person suffering from insanity (not a clinical term) would be regarded as *amens* or suffering from amentia. It is a condition in which either temporarily or permanently the person does not enjoy the use of reason. A person who is asleep does not at that moment enjoy the use of reason; a person who is utterly intoxicated or under the influence of a serious dose of narcotics does not at that moment enjoy the full use of reason; or when under anaesthesia, or hypnosis. When a person does not have the use of reason, even if the loss is temporary, that person cannot give, or make a valid act of, consent. Consent is a human act and requires all that is needed for a human act, namely the exercise of human reason.

It is interesting that in the 1917 Code amentia was not specifically mentioned as a ground for nullity of marriage. However, that did not mean that it was not used. It featured within the jurisprudence of the Courts. It was based on the premise that no valid act could take place without the use of sufficient reason; and by definition and understanding, amentia meant precisely the lack of sufficient use of reason. The 1983 Code tidied up this anomaly under the canon already referred to, as well as adding two more areas to be treated as grounds for nullity.

Clearly, this is an area where the medical sciences are involved, and it is therefore useful to add a word here about mental disorder. It is generally accepted that there are three broad divisions of mental disorder; namely psychosis, neurosis and personality disorder.

Psychoses can be found in a number of forms, but the two most widely occurring are psychotic affective disorder and schizophrenia. Psychosis is a progressive condition. In the first stage, not much may appear to be amiss; indeed the condition may appear to be very similar to neurosis. The condition may take many years to progress to the next stage, if at all. On the other hand, the transition from the first to second stage may be quite sudden and even dramatic, for example, in puerperal psychosis brought on by childbirth. The second stage is characterised by notable intellectual and volitional deterioration, but there can still be lucid spells or periods of apparent intermission. The terminal, or third stage, is total mental ruin, insanity in common parlance, though many sufferers never reach this stage.

The two forms of this sickness mentioned above were psychotic affective disorders and schizophrenia. A psychotic affective disorder is characterised by periods of mania, or euphoria, and depression, or melancholia, or (less often) in mood swings between the one and the other, which is termed a manic-depressive state (cyclothymic). Mania is identified in enthusiasm, hyperactivity, hallucinations, flights of ideas (a rapid series of uncoordinated thoughts) and the like. Depression is shown in deep sadness; despair; fear, sometimes accompanied by physical symptoms such as rapid heartbeat, hyperventilation and stomach trouble. This is not usually continuous and there are periods of remission when the person can function quite well. But once the condition has developed, then even during periods of remission the person is only barely in touch with reality, and moreover, the ability to think and to exercise the will is gravely compromised.

The other form of psychosis is schizophrenia. This is regarded as the separation between the basic structures of the personality, intellect, emotions and will, so that these are no longer co-ordinated. In every-day speech schizophrenia is often described as a Jekyll and Hyde personality. However, this manifestation is not schizophrenia, but more akin to the mood swings of a manic-depressive.

Many experts prefer not to use these terms and simply describe the symptoms that may constitute the condition.

Such symptoms include confused thought-processes, delusions and hallucinations; emotional responses to persons and to things become flat and negative; although at times there may also be periods of extreme irritability and aggression. There may be progressive loss of desire for relationships with others, and of interest in work and play; contradictary responses to persons and things, such as love and hate, pursuit or avoidance, and so on. Schizophrenia is commonly divided into four categories, simple, hebephrenic, catatonic and paranoid, according to which of these symptoms predominate. There are, of course, a variety of other forms of mental sickness under the general heading of psychosis, but the above two categories are the ones most frequently encountered in marriage nullity cases. Nonetheless, the principles which follow cover the whole range of psychotic illness. The area of psychosis is the one properly covered by the term 'amentia' although neurosis and personality disorder are two areas which will be considered under the next two grounds.

The basic question that faces the judges in any nullity case is whether the person concerned had the ability to consent, or whether the condition from which he suffered removed that ability: that is to say, was the person able to exercise his will, freely, to consent to the marriage in question?

All that we can do here is to state some of the principles to which ecclesiastical judges have to conform when they are considering such cases. Once amentia has been shown to have existed both before and after the marriage, it may be presumed that the same state of amentia existed at the time of the marriage. There is a presumption *against* the existence of a lucid interval at the time of the wedding. Although it is possible that a person may have been psychotic before the marriage, and shown to have been psychotic after the marriage, it is theoretically possible that he may have recovered sufficiently at the time of the marriage apparently to give consent. But since this possibility is so remote, and on occasion would seem to run directly contrary to the best established psychological opinion, the law presumes that lucid intervals do not occur, at least not such as to render the consent sufficient. Medical science has demonstrated that when a person is psychotic there can be, at some stage, a remission or disappearance of the symptoms of the illness. However, it is maintained that this does not mean that the disease itself has disappeared, merely that the symptoms have submerged for the time being. It would obviously be wrong to assume that a lucid interval did occur. However, even if a lucid interval had occurred, it would be extremely doubtful that the consent would have been any more effective during the period of remission than during the time of the purest manifestation of the symptoms.

On the other hand, it is also drawn from canonical jurisprudence that mental derangement appearing *after* the marriage does not necessarily mean that the same illness in fact existed *before* the marriage. This must be proved. It will be appreciated that the fact of committal to a mental institution does not necessarily mean that the person was unable to consent. There are, of course, very strict laws about the procedure of the committal of persons to mental institutions, but neither compulsory nor voluntary hospitalisation automatically mean that a person was unable to consent to marriage. Again, judges have to be guided by the opinions provided by psychiatric experts. But a note of caution is sounded by Rotal jurisprudence. It is stated quite clearly that the decision as to the invalidity of the marriage rests with the judges and not with the medical experts. Though careful attention must be paid to expert opinion, nonetheless, because a doctor is not an ecclesiastical judge, it is not his role to decide on the validity of the marriage as such. Then again, it is important that the statements of witnesses should be considered most carefully. For example, when considering the evidence of ordinary witnesses, a careful distinction must be drawn between the routine or habitual actions of the person concerned, those that require little or no mental exertion, and the other actions which demand a sane and deliberate act of will.

Finally, two things may be said in connection with the ground of amentia. Firstly, the actual consideration and evaluation of evidence about such a condition is principally determined by the constant practice of the Courts, both local and Rotal. This constant practice, or jurisprudence, must take into account the best information available from the medical and psychiatric sciences, as well as the application of such information to the basic principle that consent makes the marriage. Where it can be established that due to whatever condition, the person in question was unable to bring a sound and whole mind to the act of consent, the marriage would be regarded as null and void.

The other point to be made here is that if it can be shown that a person suffered from a mental condition pre-existing the marriage, and this condition reappeared after the marriage, then it is always worthwhile approaching the diocesan Tribunal for the consideration of the fact by canon lawyers. For obvious reasons it is not necessary to give a case to illustrate amentia.

Lack of Due Discretion

The Church and great Catholic writers have always spoken of marriage as being an event of supreme importance in the lives of the individuals concerned, as well as to society. If the teaching of the Church is that in appropriate circumstances marriage is a sacrament and permanent 'until death do us part', it must rank as one of the most important and significant events of human life. Indeed one whimsical writer said that marriage is as significant in its effects as suicide. Despite his flippancy, he had a point!

Catholic writers have, therefore, seen that if the act of marrying is so important, then the strength and the nature of the consent which must bring marriage into being must have a proportionate gravity or significance. This is what was described as the proportionality between the act of marriage and the process which must precede the actual wedding.

Marriage as a state of life is, and indeed must be, supported by a whole battery of assumptions, the chief of which is that of validity; a marriage is presumed to be valid until it is proved to be invalid. This one presumption (can.1060) of course involves a whole set of bases. For example, assumptions are made about the general capacity of an adult to marry, about the person's level of knowledge, of freedom, of intention, and so on. All these, of course, cede to proof to the contrary. But, as it will be expected, evidence to the contrary can be difficult to find, and in the absence of such evidence, the presumption of validity prevails.

Historically within the Church, such assumptions have almost always been based on what was called scholastic psychology – something which dated from the mediaeval writers. This involved a concept which may look rather simplistic today, of how a human act was performed. Briefly, a person comes to know something through his intellect; this is then seen as something good; and the will then reaches out and grasps the thing perceived as good. Assuming that this process was accompanied by the necessary freedom from external forces, this was the pattern by which a person gave consent to a marriage. However, with the development of the behavioural sciences, it became more and more clear that this expression of the psychology of human actions was a little too simple, and took no account of the forces or influences from within and without. Added to this, there was a concurrent and considerable development of the Church's own thinking about marriage. A considerable advance was made towards the end of the last century by an Encyclical of Pope Pius XI, *Casti Connubii*, and the process continued into this century. Part of the development took place in the jurisprudence of the Church's marriage Courts, in particular that of the Roman Rota, especially in the 1940s. The process was eventually crowned in the Church's understanding of marriage, now far more personalised that ever before, in the teaching of one of the Second Vatican Council's documents, *Gaudium et Spes* ('The Church in the Modern World'); and also in the Encyclical *Humanae Vitae* of Pope Paul VI of 1968.

It was *Gaudium et Spes* (no.48) that said: 'The intimate partnership of life and love which constitutes the married state [has been] established by the Creator and endowed by him with its own proper laws'. The hitherto simple notion of contract (which was obvious to all and widespread in human experience, established by the consent of the partners whose prime object was the exchange of rights over each other's bodies to acts of their nature 'apt for the generation of children') had now developed into a much more complex and elevated set of notions.

In the meantime, the jurisprudence of the Roman Rota had been exploring the whole concept of 'proportionality' called for in marriage consent, and began to use again a much older term 'discretion of judgement' to describe the proportion between the process before the marriage and the actual marriage itself. After the Council, much work was done on the revision of the Code of Canon Law; and the Consultors gradually began to put together the concepts of *Gaudium et Spes* and those derived from Rotal jurisprudence; and eventually decided upon the formula for the law in this particular area, stating that a person was unable validly to contract marriage who suffers from a grave lack of discretionary judgement concerning the essential matrimonial rights and obligations to be mutually given and accepted (cf. can.1095 n.2)

Discretion of judgement means, in simple terms, a process of reflection which has taken place prior to making a decision. Such a decision must include those elements which are calculated to involve 'the true good of the human being'; that is, it must be related to the person's well-being and fulfilment, not only in this life, but also in eternity; and by the very fact that we are speaking here of marriage, it must take into account the true well-being of the other party as well. Thus, not only will this decision contribute to *my* present and future well-being, but also to *hers*; and this must take into account the persons involved, their qualities and gifts. This is part of the 'critical' faculty, or the judgement proportionate to the importance of the act of marriage.

What has been said so far provides a background or context of the Church's law in this area. It must be said at once that however complicated this sounds, it is in ordinary circumstances, precisely and exactly what a well integrated and adequately mature young couple do when they marry. All this is generally done partly unconsciously, and partly consciously. The decision to step off the kerb and to cross the road also takes into account a number of these elements: the act of deciding to step off the kerb is equally done partly consciously and partly unconsciously, but if the act of judgement were not made, then (assuming there was on-coming traffic) the act would be injudicious and probably lead to a road accident!

Entry into marriage should not be thought to call for superhuman psychological resources of maturity and gravity. It calls for a proportionate judgement which human-beings of an adequate age and maturity of judgement can bring and always do, and always have done. But the present ground of nullity, lack of due discretion, involves precisely those elements which show that the person did not, or could not, make this required critical judgement prior to the marriage.

It is now necessary to show which elements affect this ability to make a critical judgement, that is, those things that might identify that lack of due discretion or be the cause of grave lack of discretion. For ease of explanation, these causes can be seen as either of intrinsic or extrinsic origin.

Causes which can be regarded as intrinsic might

95

include a person's gross and persistent lack of self-awareness. He may very well have a sufficient, indeed detailed, knowledge of marriage, but not apply these realities to the union in question. Another way of putting this would be to say that the person's emotional immaturity was such as to preclude him, at least at that stage, from making this necessary judgement. Extrinsic causes too can affect or even remove a person's critical faculty, such as pressure or confusion or doubt created by external circumstances. This would indicate a basic lack of internal freedom which affects the ability to make the required judgement.

It will at once be obvious that such an ability to make a judgement is not something peculiar to the Church's teaching or to ecclesiastical jurisprudence. For example, a 12-year-old boy may have inherited millions. However, civil law does not regard him as competent to make dispositions about this inheritance at that age. This is not because the civil law is perverse in that boy's particular case: it is because the law does not regard his judgement at that age competent to make important decisions.

The essence of this particular ground, therefore, is the ability to evaluate what is involved in marriage, taken alongside the two parties' qualities and attributes. But here it must also be established that the competence has to be in the marital area. It is well known to Tribunal judges that a person can have a very considerable degree of competence, indeed of judgmental ability, in the area of his work or profession, but still lack the discretionary power needed for marriage.

Some causes have already been mentioned. But some psychiatric disorders may also contribute to nullity under this ground. The clinical explanations of such disorders are given in the next section of this chapter but in certain circumstances, psychopathy, hysteria, even neuroses, may be the cause of the lack of due discretion.

It has been noted under 'amentia' that the assistance of psychiatric experts is invaluable. This is also the case in the present ground. But it should be emphasised when a psychiatrist is invited to give an expert opinion, this opinion is sought upon the nature, diagnosis, even prognosis, of some particular disorder. The expert is neither invited nor allowed to comment on the validity of the marriage: this is not his role. Moreover, as has already been said, a psychiatric tag such as 'schizophrenia' or 'psychopathy' may not be taken as a ground for nullity. In the present case the ground for nullity is the lack of due discretion. The psychological or psychiatric information can only ever form a *part* of the basis for the decision of the judges.

Examples of Lack of Due Discretion

Patrick and Paula

Patrick *was just 17 when he met* **Paula**; *she was nearly 17. Both were fairly wild; they both left school around the age of 16. He had lazed around, not much helped by his own family background; and he had already been in trouble with the police for some wild prank. Paula worked, but she regarded her wages as entirely intended to allow her to keep up with fashion in dress. The couple began going out with each other in a desultory fashion, just as they did with other partners as well. The only special characteristic of their association with each other was having intercourse every time they met. Paula, not surprisingly, became pregnant; and she was with reasonable accuracy able to determine that Patrick was the father. She in no way took fright at the pregnancy; indeed she regarded it as a rather novel experience, finding herself the centre of her friends' attention. Patrick acted as if nothing had happened. Only after some months did someone suggest to Paula that it might be an idea to get married. She thought this was a good idea. Patrick said he thought it would be fun; and so with parental permission they were married, he aged 17 and 8 months and she being aged 17 and 2 months; and five months pregnant! Neither had any money saved; but her mother gave them a room in her* *house. Some days after the marriage, Patrick decided to get a job and earn some money. Paula continued her work in a hairdressing establishment. Neither of them paid anything to Paula's mother for their keep; and both continued to behave as they had before the marriage. When Patrick began to earn some money he spent much of it on drink and betting. He also continued seeing other girls after the marriage, just as he had right up to the time of the wedding.*

When Paula went into hospital to have the baby, Patrick managed to visit her there once, though he was not on hand to take her to hospital. When she came out with the baby, Patrick was much taken with the new experience of being a father, but this did not last for long, and he returned to his friends, to drink and to the betting shop. However, by this time Paula began to take her responsibilities as a mother rather more seriously. When eventually she remonstrated with Patrick for not helping with the baby or bringing home any money, since she herself was not working, he was quite unable to see any reason at all for changing his ways. Finally, Paula's mother, thinking that the only thing to bring Patrick to his senses was go give him a jolt, put both of them and the baby out of their room. Paula, not Patrick, set to to find alternative accommodation. When she found some rooms, Patrick promised to 'do them up', but he never got round to it. Patrick produced money for a few weeks for rent and food, but then stopped. When Paula started to nag him to 'pull up his socks', he told her he was bored with her and left her to live in his parents' home. That was last she saw of him. Some time later, Paula obtained a divorce with a view to trying to ensure maintenance from Patrick, but even that was sporadic. She then met a Catholic, and as a result, petitioned for a decree of nullity so as to marry him. The grounds alleged were the lack of due discretion on the part of her previous husband, Patrick, her child's father. Evidence of Patrick's crass immaturity was brought forward in abundance to prove the grounds; and a decree of nullity was granted.

Ariadne and Harper

Ariadne, *a Catholic, came from a far from ordinary background. Her mother was unhealthily religious, claiming all manner of prophetic and quasi-magical powers. She had been in several concentration camps and had promised God an act of self-sacrifice by way of thanksgiving for her survival. This involved, as it turned out, marriage to a crippled sailor whom she had previously never met. The consequent upbringing of Ariadne was affected by a situation of appalling marital discord, accompanied by a disposition towards piosity on the part of the mother. Ariadne went off to a Polytechnic with relics strung around her neck; and she stood out as a marked eccentric in the social circles at college. Her mother was extremely anxious that she should marry. In these circumstances, Ariadne met a much older post-graduate, **Harper**, of curious looks and with known lecherous morals. He was some 15 years older than Ariadne. By this time, as a very mature student, he had acquired a strong antipathy to religion in general and to Catholicism in particular. He ogled the petitioner (as he did all the other girls in the college); but Ariadne took this as a mark of very acceptable flattery. She invited him to her home; the mother baked special cakes intended to guarantee the success of the relationship. Within two weeks, Ariadne approached the college Chaplain who refused to have anything to do with the marriage; and she then pursued the Curate in the local parish church, who agreed to marry the couple, though with considerable doubts (which were recorded in the marriage dossier). The marriage took place, when she was 25 and he was 40, approximately six weeks after they first met. The common life, which only lasted 10 months, was disastrous. He continued to seek the company of other women; refused to have children (a decision he disclosed after the marriage); made it difficult for Ariadne to practice her faith. Through all this, Ariadne was convinced she could convert and change Harper. Then Harper went* *beserk, offered considerable violence to Ariadne and her mother, so the girl left him. There was sufficient evidence from the neighbours (about Adriadne's home background), and from college students (about the time before and after the marriage), to show that both Ariadne and Harper were lacking in due discretion; and a decree of nullity was issued (together with a restrictive clause on both).*

Inability to Assume the Obligations of Marriage

Previous sections considered a person's ability or inability to make the necessary critical judgement about the rights and obligations to be assumed in marriage. However, beyond this critical judgement, there is also the matter of a person's *ability* to assume these obligations. It is possible to conceive of a situation where a person can make the required critical judgement, but for other reasons be quite unable to assume these obligations. An analogy (and no analogy is perfect) would be the person who makes the necessary judgement, that is to say does not lack due discretion, but finds after the marriage that he is impotent. The point of the analogy is to highlight the distinction that could exist between a person's discretionary power and his ability to assume the obligations of marriage (in a sense much wider than intercourse).

The essential obligations of marriage are permanence, fidelity and openness to children; but in addition, there are those elements which call for union between the couple at an emotional, sexual, psychological, relational, as well as intellectual level. As well as the traditional obligations, there are today those which involve the 'good of the spouses' or the 'community of life and love'; that is to say the ability to form and sustain an inter-personal relationship on the marital level. The Code of Canon Law now enshrines this ground (which the 1917 Code did not) at can.1095 n.3. This indicates that no-one who is unable, for causes of psychological nature, to assume the essential obligations of marriage can validly contract marriage.

We have already briefly looked at some details of a psychiatric nature which were relevant to the ground of amentia. These concern defined psychoses. It would help here to consider the areas of neurosis and personality disorder. These relate to the requirement of the canon when it speaks of the 'causes of a psychological nature'.

To begin with, the category of sickness referred to as neurosis concerns a chronic disorder, usually extremely distressing for the sufferer. It is distinguished not just *quantitatively* from psychosis, but also *qualitatively*. It is characterised by recurrent attacks of anxiety (anxiety neurosis or neurasthenia), obsession or compulsion (obsessive compulsive neurosis or psychasthenia), unreasonable fears (phobias) or unexplained or neurological symptoms (hysteria). The manifestation of these symptoms is quite commonplace, for example in an *anxiety* neurosis there is, of course, an onslaught of anxiety; sometimes accompanied by laboured breathing, palpitations and the like. This can be quite serious although it generally passes quickly. It has no long-term effect on the mental processes.

In the case of an *obsessional* neurosis, there is an onset of persistent and unwanted ideas or impulses which cannot be escaped. These frequently lead to compulsions like the constant washing of hands. The person may or may not recognise the pointlessness of the obsession or compulsion, but is acutely aware of wanting to escape the situation. This struggle causes great suffering and often isolates a person from his family. While the psychological pain can be intense on the emotional level, the mind remains clear in areas not related to the obsession or compulsion.

A phobia involves continuous and intense unreasonable fear of a particular object. It is often sporadic; and the intellect and will are unaffected except in connection with the object of the phobia. But it can be the prelude to a more serious disorder. With hysteria there are frequent and dramatic bodily or neurological symptoms, temporary deafness for example, accompanied sometimes by very colourful or dramatic language and posturing. It is not at all easy in such cases to determine what is genuine and what is affected. In true hysteria there can be a serious disturbance of the consciousness, but of a transitory nature. In general, there is a presumption that outside the area of the neurosis, the mental functions are normal.

Personality disorders were relatively late (in the last century) in being described. Psychopathy is one of the gravest. This is described as an unhealthy psychic condition manifested by abnormal behaviour in persons who are neither psychotic nor neurotic. Of course, it is not easy to define what is normal and what is abnormal behaviour outside a particular social context. There is a problem of terminology which must be confronted. Generally speaking the term 'psychopathy' can be applied to the whole category; whereas those who cause actual harm to others are sometimes referred to, especially in North America, as 'sociopaths'.

Psychopaths may manifest some of the symptoms of psychosis or even neurosis. Indeed the condition may even be the precursor of something more serious. Basically, it is their *behaviour* which is abnormal; and this may well lead to the conclusion that there must be something wrong mentally; often something very wrong in terms of emotional function. But it is important to stress that they are in no way out of touch with reality, or even impaired in thinking or willing. Therefore this condition tends to be more associated with inability, rather than amentia or the lack of due discretion.

With regard to the application of jurisprudential considerations to these psychiatric problems, the question to be asked by the judges in any particular case is whether the condition makes it *impossible* for the person to assume the essential obligations of marriage.

Some of the points which the judges must take into account are:

- Is the psychological problem rooted in the personality?
- Is it serious?

- Was it actually present in the person at the time of the marriage?
- Did it actually affect the consent given at the time of the marriage?

An affirmative answer to each of these questions goes a long way to establishing the ground of nullity. Moreover, the judges must be satisfied that the problem itself was not caused by the experience of married life, and it is not a later reaction to the marital situation.

Jurists also ask whether the condition, as existing at the time of marriage, is perpetual. The received opinion about this is that although the perpetuity of the condition is helpful evidence, it is by no means a necessity to conclude the inability to assume the obligations of marriage.

Two examples are given below. These broadly involve psychopathy and hysteria. However, remembering that psychiatric diagnoses are not in themselves grounds of nullity, there are other serious areas of psychiatric concern affecting marriage including sexual inadequacy, alcoholism, homosexuality, sadism, hyperaesthesia, trans-sexualism, nyphomania, among many others.

Examples of Inability to Assume the Obligations of Marriage

Angela and Roland: psychopathy

Angela met **Roland** at the 21st birthday party of her sister. At this time she was 23 and Roland was 24. He was tall, handsome, very charming, though inclined to be a little distant at times. The couple saw each other a few times a week for a period of a year. He appeared to be kind and attentive, and very polite to her parents. He seemed to have plenty of money, though he was always reticent about where he worked and what he did; but Angela concluded that he had something to do with selling cars. The courtship progressed and they became engaged. Only two events caused any disturbance during this time. One was at the time the couple had selected an engagement ring,

Roland had collected it from the jewellers, leaving the car parked in the street. On returning to the car he said he had found it had been broken into and the ring stolen. In any event they were able to make a claim on his car insurance for the price of the ring. The other event was when Roland had had several drinks at a party, and had become very aggressive and unpleasant to his own brother who had been larking about. The wedding went off well; but on the honeymoon Roland discovered that he had left his wallet behind with all their money. However, Angela was able to pay the bill with her credit cards, which sums Roland was to return to her when they got home. On the honeymoon, Roland did not seem to be very gentle at intercourse, but Angela put this down to his (and her) inexperience. On returning home, the couple set about painting and decorating their newly acquired flat; and it was at this time that Angela discovered that Roland had left his job. He said it was because he wanted to look for something with more future as well as more money. Whilst he was looking for a suitable job, Angela was working and supporting them both. Roland did not seem to be in any great hurry to find a job, although she put this down to the fact that he was anxious to find the right one. Nonetheless, she suggested to him that perhaps for the time being he might take any job that would bring in some money, and meanwhile continue to look for the right job, answering advertisements and the like. Roland did not think this was the right approach at all; but he then discovered what he thought would be the ideal work – collaborating with a man who was writing a film script. He therefore began working at home. He asked Angela to lend him £250 to put into the venture as his share of the capital. She felt that to eat into their savings in this way would be unwise and gently refused. At this stage he became violent; and indeed on every subsequent occasion when he could not get his own way, he resorted to violence.

He had also started staying out at night, and for periods

of several days at a stretch. He accounted for his absences by telling Angela that he was working with his partner on selecting shooting locations for the forthcoming film. Knowing nothing of the film business, she believed him to start with; but then his general attitude towards her, his violence, the fact that he was not earning anything at all (although apparently able to find money for drinking and eating meals away from home) – all this began to make her doubt him. Occasions of violence were followed by episodes of deep remorse, with assurances that he would do better in the future. However, the situation at home was becoming desperate; and then Angela became pregnant. This seemed to anger Roland even more and his violence towards her, even in that condition, increased. She threatened to leave him, and there was a further scene with tears in which he protested that he could not live without her. He even threatened suicide if she left him. Finally the time came when she had to leave work, and there was still no sign of him improving; so she did indeed leave him and returned to her parents. He took to haunting the parents' home, threatening alternately violence to his wife and her parents, or suicide. Eventually, the police had to be called to restrain him. Subsequently, Angela divorced Roland, alleging cruelty and unreasonable behaviour and then petitioned for a decree of nullity, alleging Roland's inability to assume the obligations of marriage. The story she told was corroborated to the hilt, the grounds approved and a decree was issued.

Charles and Daphne: hysteria

Charles *met* **Daphne** *at a New Year's Eve Ball. The couple began to go out together; and Charles was deeply attracted by the girl. She was very beautiful, dressed extremely well, in the fashion, but she was not unknown to 'dress to attract' wearing fairly low-cut blouses and very close-fitting dresses. She was the life and soul of the party and invariably had a circle of male admirers in*

105

attendance on such occasions. She was a forthright girl and spoke her mind. All this appeared to Charles to be very captivating. His sister, who met Daphne, took an instant dislike to her, but could not tell her brother why.

In many ways Daphne appeared to be flirty and coquettish, and was quite ready to have intercourse with Charles before marriage. An engagement took place; there were a few rows between the couple (on one occasion Daphne threw the ring back at Charles over some tiny incident, of no apparent importance whatsoever). After the marriage, the couple went on their honeymoon, but from the very start she did not appear to be keen on the intimacies of married life; and indeed after only two occasions of intercourse on the honeymoon, it became infrequent. Charles also noticed that Daphne appeared to be very jealous of him from the start; he did not give her cause for this, but she would act in a jealous and suspicious fashion when he so much as gave the time of day to a member of the opposite sex in their hotel.

When they returned home from their honeymoon to their newly acquired flat, Charles was pleased to see that Daphne immediately took up with one of their neighbours and was very close to her. However, he was very surprised when he returned home one day to hear Daphne referring to her close friend and neighbour in bitter and spiteful terms. It emerged that the two women had had a small disagreement about the shopping; and from that moment onwards Daphne cut the neighbour and refused to speak to her. At the same time, Daphne took up with another neighbour and was extremely close to her; but that friendship also soon ended. The situation with the neighbours now became extremely embarrassing. If Charles was observed by Daphne to bid good-morning to either of them she refused to speak to him for several days. Eventually, Charles had to think of moving their flat to escape the embarrassment.

Daphne acted strangely in other ways as well. She appeared to suffer from very frequent aches and pains; and an especially painful neck. Doctors were consulted and no help could be given; until finally one consultant suggested seeing a neurologist or a psychiatrist as he doubted that there was anything physically wrong with Daphne. This infuriated her, and she refused to see the consultant again, even darkly hinting at some impropriety that he had committed when she last saw him. Apart from all this, the relationship between the married couple had become impossible. In a sunny mood, Daphne could change in a flash; and Charles never knew when he returned home in the evening how he would find her. When they did have rows, Daphne raised her voice to such a pitch that her husband feared that she might become hysterical. Finally he discovered that she was having a relationship with an insurance agent who collected at the door. This was the last straw for Charles and he took advice from his doctor as well as a priest. Both told him that in their view he would never be able to live with Daphne; and advised him to leave her before his own health, which had begun to suffer, broke down completely. Subsequently, a divorce was granted to Daphne; and Charles petitioned for a decree of nullity on the grounds of Daphne's inability to assume the obligations of marriage. Evidence showed that she was childish, immature, spoiled; that she suffered from a serious hysterical personality disorder. In the light of evidence that this was a condition from which she had suffered from before the marriage, the grounds were found to be proved; and a decree of nullity granted.

Chapter Six

DIRIMENT IMPEDIMENTS

MOST people have some idea of what a diriment, or nullifying impediment is; for example, they would appreciate that a man cannot marry his sister. In everyday terms, this would be ruled out because the law of the land says so: 'diriment impediment' is a technical expression in the Church's law for such an embargo. An impediment is some fact or situation which prohibits two specific people from marrying each other. If such a marriage takes place without a 'dispensation' (if one could be granted), the union is invalid.

The Church like the state has specific rules about impediments; and has its own list of them. It will be appreciated that impediments in civil law are now generally far fewer than those which exist in Canon Law; although, of course, the civil impediments derive their origin from the earlier law of the Church. Some of the Church's diriment impediments are regarded as being solely of ecclesiastical law and therefore can usually be dispensed; others are regarded as being derived from the Divine positive law and these cannot be dispensed by the Church. The Church was founded by Christ as a means of redemption and grace for all mankind and as a means through which the sacraments are conferred. The Church was also established by Christ to administer these sacraments; and therefore the Church has the power to establish rules and regulations for the administration and the reception of the sacraments. Marriage is a sacrament and is therefore subject to the regulations of the Church in this regard. It is the Church which determines which impediments are derived from the Divine positive law, and which establishes other impediments in its law for reasons of fitness or suitability, and for the good of its members.

For a couple to be married in the Catholic Church, they are required to go through an investigation called a 'prenuptial enquiry'. The purpose of this is to determine, among other things, that they are free to marry in the Church, that is, free of any diriment impediment. If an impediment of ecclesiastical law does come to light which the Church can dispense, and there is a dispensation, the marriage can be celebrated validly in the Church.

It may occasionally happen that an impediment is not known about before the marriage; the marriage takes place; and the impediment is discovered afterwards. Assuming the couple are still together, and assuming the impediment is one that can be dispensed, and the Church does dispense it, the couple would be required to renew their consent before a priest and two witnesses; and would then be regarded as validly married. However, if the marriage has broken down, the couple are separated and divorced, and the dispensation was undispensed, then a procedure could take place to show the invalidity of the marriage.

It should be noted that according to the Church's law, non-Catholics are not bound to ecclesiastical laws of the Church (can.11). But, of course, they are bound by those regulations deriving from what the Church regards as Divine positive law.

Where there is an undispensed diriment impediment and there is a broken marriage and divorce, there are two procedures by which the matter can be dealt with to show invalidity; one is a formal process; the other is an informal or administrative process. The latter process is one that can be used when all the facts of the case can be established by certain and authentic documents. Both these forms of procedure will be dealt with later. This chapter deals with the spread of diriment impediments, divided into those which may require a formal nullity procedure; and those which certainly can be dealt with by the administrative procedure.

Diriment Impediments Which May Require Proof by Formal Nullity Process

Age

The current law of the Church stipulates that a valid marriage cannot be contracted by a boy until he has passed his 16th birthday and a girl until she has passed her 14th birthday. (can.1083,§1) This law hardly affects persons in England and Wales, where in civil law no marriage may take place before either party is 16, and even after this parental permission is required up to the age of 18, or in the United States, where in many States parental consent is required up to 21. In this respect the practical rule is that for a marriage of Catholics the civil law must be observed. As a matter of interest, the 1983 Code of Canon Law obviously appreciates that 16 and 14 are very young ages indeed. But of course as a universal law it has to take account of customs which exist throughout the world, and not just in the Western Church. However, the law also states that a Conference of Bishops may establish an older age for marriage, although the Conference may not establish a diriment impediment; only the Holy See may establish such impediments (cf can.1083,§2).

In different parts of the world, different civil laws apply. It is necessary, therefore, to appreciate that there are some places in which marriage can take place (civilly) even before the age of 16. But the canonical rule applies only to Catholics since it is regarded that this rule is one of ecclesiastical law. The natural law requires that the parties have sufficient knowledge and discretionary ability concerning the obligations of marriage, as well as the ability to assume them, in order to marry validly. Though non-Catholics are not bound by the laws of the Church, they are bound by the requirements of natural law. Hence, if these requirements were not fulfilled, the person would be able to pursue a nullity case on these grounds. If the person was unbaptised, then a different procedure might be used (see Chapter 9). Insofar as the

111

impediment is one of ecclesiastical law, it can be dispensed by the Church, but this would have to be for an extremely serious reason, and of course, it must be remembered that the civil law would not permit marriages to take place below its required minimum age.

Abduction or Detention

This is rare, but not unknown. The law states that no marriage may take place between a man and woman who has been abducted or detained with a view to contracting marriage with her. A marriage may take place when the woman has been released, returned to a safe and free place, and *then* freely decides to marry the man (can.1089).

The use of the two words abduction and detention is merely to distinguish between the woman being *taken away* on the one hand; or being *kept* or *held* in a place to which she would not go voluntarily. Therefore, the abduction or detention must have been with a view to marriage being arranged. This must have been the original motive for the abduction or the detention. The concept of the abduction or detention involves violence: it must have been against the women's will in the first place. Thus, if the girl elopes willingly, even against the will of her parents, this impediment would not apply.

The impediment is of ecclesiastical law; but it will be seen that the law in no way envisages dispensation. The only way in which the impediment ceases is by means of the girl being returned to a safe place which is quite outside the power of the one abducting or detaining her. When she is entirely free from this influence, she may then decide to marry or not as she chooses.

Crime

This term is misleading since in Canon Law it has a very specific meaning. There are two forms of this impediment. Both, it will be seen at once, are intended to preserve the social fabric as well as the sanctity of marriage. One form of the impediment concerns a person who kills his own spouse so as to marry another person; or kills the spouse of the other person, again with a view to marriage with the survivor (can.1090,§1). Following this act, the impediment of crime then exists which precludes the murderer from marrying the survivor. It is necessary that the killing is done with a view to the marriage. And the killing must, of course, be intentional; for example, it would not apply if a man was driving, had an accident and his wife was killed in the crash. This would not be within the scope of this canon unless the crash was intentional with a view to killing the wife so as to marry another woman. The same applies to a man deliberately killing the husband of the women he wants to marry.

The other form of this impediment involves conspiracy between the couple who wish to marry. The Code says: 'They also invalidly attempt marriage with each other, who by mutual physical or moral action, bring about the death of either's spouse' (can.1090,§2). The canon speaks of: 'bringing about the death' of the spouse of either. This is wider than killing in the technical sense. That is, it is not necessary that the couple actually shoot or knife the victim! For example, say the guilty couple plan a shock for the victim. They know the victim suffers from angina, and is likely to have a heart attack at the slightest shock. The guilty couple engineer a shock to the victim, when they themselves are well away from the scene. Although the ensuing death may be due to some kind of cardiac arrest, the couple would still be guilty through their mutual action of bringing about the death, and the impediment would arise.

This impediment is also one of ecclesiastical law; but the Church would be extremely circumspect about dispensing an impediment, especially if there were to be public knowledge of the facts, even though no specific charge of homicide cold be brought against the couple. It will also be observed that the point of listing this impediment (as also others under this chapter) is as follows. Usually the guilty couple would marry anyway with the undisclosed impediment. Assuming that the marriage breaks down and one of the parties then wishes to marry again, the undispensed impediment of crime would have to be established in an ecclesiastical Court so as to obtain a decree of nullity. It will be appreciated that this is hardly something that can be established by means of documentary evidence.

Public propriety

This is another impediment that originates in ecclesiastical law. It arises from an invalid marriage, and it can also arise from 'public or notorious concubinage'. It is an impediment which is very like that of affinity (with which we will deal shortly) and it invalidates a marriage between a man and the mother or daughter of the woman with whom he is living. An example illustrates the impediment. David is living with (or married invalidly, by reason of some impediment, to) Helen. There is an impediment to marriage if, later on, David tries to contract a union with Helen's mother or daughter. In technical terms, marriage is prohibited and invalidated between David and the blood relations of Helen (with whom he is living) in the direct line in the first degree. (can.1093). We will see how the relationship between two people is calculated in the direct and collateral lines when we deal with consanguinity and affinity.

The impediment will arise between two people who are bound to the form of marriage, for example two Catholics, who marry invalidly or publicly and notoriously live together. It is sometimes possible, for serious and grave reasons, to obtain a dispensation from this impediment. This impediment may have to be dealt with by way of the formal procedure, because witnesses may well be required to show that a couple only lived together, and were not validly married.

Impotence

Reference has already been made to the description of marriage in can.1055,§1 in which the marital partnership 'of its own very nature is ordered to the well-being of the spouses and to the procreation and upbringing of children...' Consequently, one of the elements which must accompany this statement about marriage is the ability of a couple to have sexual intercourse. This does not mean a couple *must* have sexual intercourse; it means solely that they are *able* to have intercourse. Accordingly, the law of the Church says that: 'Antecedent and perpetual impotence to have sexual intercourse, whether on the part of the man or the woman, whether absolute or relative, by its very nature invalidates marriage' (can.1084,§1).

There are a series of terms which must be defined for the purposes of this impediment: for example, what is intercourse? When is impotence antecendent and perpetual? What is absolute and relative impotence? It is necessary to explain these terms so that the law is clear.

The interpretation of these terms in particular stems from the jurisprudence of the Church. Sexual intercourse involves erection of the penis, penetration of the vagina and ejaculation therein. When this is not possible, there is no intercourse; and there is then the condition of impotence. Hence, if it is not possible for the male to have and sustain an erection, or not possible for penetration to take place, or not possible for ejaculation to take place within the vagina – these are all causes of impotence.

Additionally, if the woman has no vagina, or if it is deformed to the extent that it cannot be penetrated by the male organ, or where there is a severe case of vaginismus, involuntary spasms of the vaginal muscles which effectively bars penetration by the male member, this also amounts to impotence.

It is also required that impotence should be antecendent and perpetual. Obviously, it is necessary for the condition to have existed at the time of the marriage and if so it is regarded as having existed beforehand. Hence, it is 'ante-cendent'. However, the term 'perpetual' is to be understood in the canonical sense. This means that the condition continues and will continue and cannot be cured by ordinary means. 'Ordinary means' are those which are available to the couple within their own environment and, above all, which do not constitute a serious threat to the health or life of the person concerned.

Thus, for example, a person living in a Brazilian slum may be suffering from impotence. The condition is caused by a problem which could easily be remedied in a Harley Street Clinic; but the person cannot avail himself of the operation given his economic circumstances in Brazil. In that sense, the ordinary means are not available to him; and hence the condition is canonically perpetual.

It has already been inferred above that the condition could affect the man or the woman; but the law also indicates that the condition could be absolute or relative. It would be absolute if, for example, the man had no penis. He, obviously, could not have intercourse with anyone. Or the condition might be relative in which for some psychological reason the woman, with this particular partner, suffers from vaginismus; but with another partner she might well be able to have quite satisfactory intercourse. Therefore the condition is relative to this particular partner and situation.

There are a very wide number of physiological causes that may render a man impotent; generally there are fewer that affect a woman. It is well recognised that the cause can be organic or psychological. However, whatever the cause, if it creates the condition of impotence there is an impediment to marriage.

One point which today is not without some relevance today with the very considerable advance in surgical procedures following the McIndoe technique which was perfected during the Second World War in connection with skin grafting following facial burns. It is not at all uncommon for a woman to be born without a vagina. The success of skin grafting operations has meant that there is the possibility of creating an artificial vagina by means of skin grafting with human tissue.

A woman born without a vagina would be regarded as impotent because the construction of an artificial vagina would be regarded as employing 'extraordinary' means. However, if the woman had for some reason already had an artificial vagina constructed prior to the marriage, there would be no impediment to her marrying.

Impotence is regarded as an impediment of the natural law; and obviously cannot be dispensed. However, it is important to note that sterility is not an impediment to marriage. Likewise there is no impediment for a woman who has passed the change of life (cf can.1084,§3). The point here is that the technical definition of intercourse can be realised in all these cases; and hence the concept of impotence does not apply.

Proof of impotence is obviously not easy. In general, it will for obvious reasons be difficult to obtain evidence from a time before the marriage. The assistance of medical experts is therefore especially important. It is because of this difficulty that the law has a further disposition which is usually of considerable help. A person alleging impotence would also obviously have to allege that there had never been intercourse; and therefore that the marriage had never been consummated. There is a special provision in the Code which says that a nullity case introduced on the grounds of impotence may be transferred from that kind of procedure to the special procedure for seeking a dispensation from an unconsummated marriage (cf can.1681).

Finally, the law has one further point to make. It is this. Prior to a marriage there can obviously be doubt as to whether a person is impotent in the canonical sense. If there is such a doubt, the person may not be prevented from marrying – he must be given the benefit of the doubt. But equally, if the marriage has taken place, and the doubt still remains as to whether the person is impotent or not, the marriage cannot be declared null and void whilst that doubt persists. That is to say that following marriage, the presumption of validity holds good in spite of the doubt; and remains until the doubt is entirely dispelled.

Diriment Impediments Which May be Dealt With by Means of the Administrative Process

Before dealing with the second group of impediments, we must mention again the reason for making the distinction between these two groups. This second group can be dealt with (to establish their existence and thereby show a marriage to be invalid) very much more easily, as will be seen in the next chapter. The procedure merely demands that the impediment is shown to exist by means of certain and authentic documents according to the special norms of the law. Bearing this point in mind, it will be seen that the following impediments are all capable of being demonstrated through written documents rather than by formal verbal evidence.

Prior marriage or 'ligamen'

A person who is bound by a valid marriage may not contract a further marriage during the lifetime of his spouse. If he does attempt a second union, it will be invalid. On the other hand, it may be possible to declare the first union to be invalid for some reason; in which case it will be possible for the person concerned to marry, provided that the nullity (or dispensation from an unconsummated union or dissolution of a non-sacramental union) has been properly established according to the laws of the Church.

This impediment appears to be most complicated when first examined, but with appropriate documentation its existence can often be declared fairly speedily. An example will illustrate the impediment. Henry married Rachel. Both are baptised non-Catholics; they marry in their local

Anglican Parish Church. The marriage is not happy and Rachel leaves Henry, divorces him and then marries – this time in a Register Office – Raymond, also a baptised non-Catholic. This marriage likewise disintegrates, and Raymond falls in love with Susan, a Roman Catholic. Provided it can be shown that Henry was validly married to Rachel, and that Henry was alive when Rachel married Raymond, it follows that there is the impediment of a prior marriage, or ligamen, which invalides the marriage of Rachel and Raymond. Hence, Raymond is free to marry Susan (can.1085,§1).

This impediment is of the Divine law, and therefore it binds everyone. In the above example, the impediment ceases to exist between Rachel and Raymond when Henry dies. Thus if Rachel and Raymond marry after Henry's death, their union would be regarded as valid. Raymond would then not be free to marry Susan. More attention will be given to this matter in the next chapter when dealing with the actual process for the establishment of the impediment.

Disparity of cult

The Church regards a valid marriage of the baptised to be a sacrament. The Church also maintains that for a sacramental marriage it is necessary for *both* the parties to be baptised, not just one party. That is to say, a marriage between one baptised person and an unbaptised person is not regarded as a sacrament, although it is regarded as valid. The exception to this is if a Catholic happens to marry, in a Catholic Church, an unbaptised person without a dispensation being granted. This union would be invalid. This is described as the impediment of disparity of cult or of worship (can.1086,§1).

The Church does allow a Catholic to marry an unbaptised person and it does so by means of dispensing the impediment of disparity of cult. The chances of of a Catholic marrying an unbaptised person in a Catholic

Church without a dispensation are remote; but sometimes it can happen. For example, an unbaptised person may have spent a lot of his time with Catholics; and even gone to Mass with them. Later on he quite innocently, but of course wrongly, describes himself as a Catholic. If the necessary (and legally stipulated) checks are not made and the union takes place in the Catholic Church, the union would *de facto* be invalid. However, the completion of the pre-nuptial enquiry should elicit the information about the person's baptismal status. The only other point here is that when a baptised non-Catholic marries an unbaptised person, if the marriage subsequently broke down this might give rise to a procedure dealt with later in connection with the dissolution of the bond in favour of the Faith (see chapter 9).

Holy Order

The basis of this impediment is that a cleric who is in major orders – the priesthood or diaconate – cannot validly marry unless the impediment has been dispensed by the appropriate authority (can.1087). The Church does dispense the impediment in case of deacons without too much difficulty. But although she also dispenses from the impediment of the priesthood, dispensation is not granted easily or readily, and it is only after the most careful examination of the case. Even so, when the Holy See has dispensed the impediment of the priesthood and thereby enabled a former priest to marry, this union, although a sacrament, and taking place with the blessing of the Church, must be celebrated quietly, without fuss and public show. The reasons are obvious.

Public perpetual vow of chastity

This impediment (can.1088) prohibits, under pain of nullity, a man or woman who has taken a public perpetual vow of chastity in a religious institute from attempting marriage. The important point here is that the vow is public and perpetual. There are other vows which are private and temporary which are not covered by this diriment impediment. The Holy See for special reasons can dispense from a public perpetual vow; and sometimes the diocesan bishop may do so.

Consanguinity

Consanguinity is the impediment which precludes the marriage of blood relations. The impediment can exist in what is called the collateral line, which is the relationship between brothers and sisters, between cousins, between uncle and niece *etc*. The relationship can also be in the direct line, which is the connection between a mother and son, or grandmother and grandson and the like. The best method of establishing the relationship that exists between two persons is to plot some kind of genealogical tree. The lines running up and down are in the direct line; those running off as branches are the collateral lines. To complicate the matter further, there are also *degrees* of relationship. For example, there is a closer relationship between brother and sister than there is between two cousins. To be able to plot the degree of relationship it is necessary to establish the common ancestor which exists in a particular case.

To give an example of consanguinity, let us say that Henry is the father of Peter and Paul. Henry is the common ancestor. The degree of relationship existing between the two brothers is determined by counting the number of generations on both sides back to, but not counting the common ancestor. Thus, in the case of Peter and Paul there is one generation back to Henry, their father, on both sides. Hence, Peter and Paul are connected in the second degree, and since this relationship is one concerning the branches stemming from the common ancestor, their relationship is in the collateral line. Then Peter and Paul have children. Peter is the father of Mary and Paul is the father of Robert. The relationship between Robert and Mary is decided by counting the generations back on *both* sides to Henry, the common ancestor. There are four such generations, two on each side, not counting Henry. Hence the relationship is described as being in the fourth degree of the collateral line.

There is an added complication where the generations back to the common ancestor are not equal. For instance, the relationship between Paul and Mary is that of uncle and niece. The way this is described in Canon Law is to count the generations on both sides. The relationship between Paul and Mary is therefore in the third degree in the collateral line. In the *direct line*, the relationship between Henry and Mary is that of the third degree in the direct line.

This is a complicated impediment, but it can easily be resolved by drawing a diagram. For example where two cousins are related not only on their father's side, but also on their mother's side. The law of the Church is that consanguinity existing in the direct line either ascending or descending constitutes a diriment impediment. In the collateral line marriage is invalid by reason of consanguinity up to the fourth degree. Marriage between any relatives in the direct line, such as mother and son, grandmother and grandson *etc.*, is invalid. In the collateral line a marriage between brother and sister, and first and second cousins is invalid. But the relationship between second or third cousins does not create a diriment impediment (can.1091).

The origin of the impediment of consanguinity depends upon the nature of the relationship. It is considered that consanguinity in the direct line is an impediment of the Divine law, in the first degree, and some authors regard other degrees also as of the Divine law, though this is not so certain. If it is not an impediment of the Divine law for these other degrees, it is most certainly an impediment of the ecclesiastical law. For these direct line relationships, the Church does not generally grant dispensations.

In the collateral line, most authors regard the

relationship between brother and sister as an impediment of Divine law; in all other degrees of the collateral line, that is, between first cousins and less, it is an impediment of the ecclesiastical law. The unbaptised are not bound by the impediments which are *certainly* considered to be merely of the ecclesiastical law. Where there exists a relationship between two non-baptised persons which is not certainly of the Divine law the impediment does not arise. Since the unbaptised are bound not by ecclesiastical law, but by the civil law of the place where they live, the point hardly need concern us here. The Church does not dispense from the impediment in the second degree of the collateral line; but she will dispense for good reasons in lesser degrees. So far as an undispensed diriment impediment of consanguinity is concerned, this is established by means of documents, usually by a combination of marriage and birth certificates.

Affinity

Affinity exists between a man and the blood relations of his wife and vice versa. Affinity in the collateral line exists between, say, a man and the collateral blood relations of his wife, for example her sisters, cousins and so on. Affinity in the direct line exists between the man and the mother and daughter (and so on, upwards and downwards) of his wife.

So far as the law of the Church is concerned, the impediment of affinity only exists in the direct line; and *in any degree* of the direct line. The law no longer regards affinity in the collateral line as an impediment. Again, it is usually a simple matter to establish the impediment in the direct line by means of marriage and birth certificates (can.1092).

Legal relationship

When a person is legally adopted, so far as the Church is concerned, there arises a relationship between the

123

adopted person and the couple adopting him or her. This works both in the direct line (the adopted person and the adoptive parent) and the collateral line (the adopted person and the natural children or blood relatives of the adoptive parent). For example, William and Mary have two children (Peter and Paula). Harry is adopted by William and Mary; and there comes into existence through the legal adoption a legal relationship between the two adoptive parents and Harry in the direct line. A legal relationship comes into existence between Harry and Peter and Paula, in the collateral line, in the second degree. The law states that a diriment impediment exists in the direct line and up to the second degree of the collateral line; hence between Harry and his adoptive parents (in the direct line); and between Harry and his adoptive brother and sister (the collateral line in the second degree) (can.1094).

For the canonical provisions to operate, there must be a *legal* relationship: a legal adoption must have taken place. It must also be noted that the ecclesiastical law here (which can be dispensed by the Church) does not necessarily follow the civil law: in some countries there is no legal relationship through adoption. Regardless of the civil law, however, the impediment binds Catholics (not non-Catholics). It should be noted that because this is a dispensation of ecclesiastical law, a marriage which took place before the present Code came into operation, so far as this impediment is concerned, would be judged according to the 1917 Code. The old law stated that the impediment was diriment in the Church where it was diriment in civil law. However, that is a refinement which would have to be dealt with by a Tribunal.

We have now concluded our examination of the impediments which invalidate marriage. The point of mentioning them here was that if a diriment impediment does exist, it may be possible to show that the marriage under examination is null and void. In the next section we will move on to examine two types of nullity procedure that exist in the Church: the formal and the administrative types of procedure. All those grounds of nullity examined in the earlier chapters, together with the first group of impediments dealt with here, are considered under the formal procedure; while the impediments mentioned in the second group above are dealt with by the administrative procedure.

Special Note About Divorce

This particular note has been placed here so as to be seen by anyone who turns on to read about the Church's nullity procedure.

There is a particularly sad, and damaging, misconception in the minds of many Catholics concerning divorce. It is sometimes thought (but quite wrongly) that if a Catholic has been divorced, then he or she is barred from the sacraments. This is quite wrong. The only situation in which a Catholic should not receive Holy Communion is when he or she is divorced *and* remarried. Much unhappiness is caused by this misconception.

Section III

EXAMINATION OF A MARRIAGE

Chapter Seven

THE TRIBUNAL AND ITS PROCEDURE

EVERY nullity case is made up of three distinct elements. There is first of all the evidence which is collected as a result of an original petition which alleges that a particular marriage is null and void. Secondly, there is the weighing of that evidence and application to it of the Church's jurisprudence. It should be reiterated here that the term jurisprudence is used in a completely different sense to the way in which it is used in civil law. In the latter, jurisprudence has the sense of the philosophy of law; in Church marriage tribunals it is used in the sense of case law. Indeed, tribunal decisions have a role in the interpretation of the law. An individual decision, or 'sentence', is regarded as being a privately binding interpretation of the law, although only binding on the parties to the case (can.16,§3). However the constant process of making decisions on various elements in connection with the nullity of marriage helps to develop the understanding and seeks to clarify concepts in regard to grounds for nullity.

The primary source for this jurisprudence is the Roman Rota and its decisions; but for reasons already noted, individual Rotal decisions in themselves are of limited value. The real assistance given by the Rotal jurisprudence is to highlight and indeed to define trends and directions of jurisprudential thinking. The other area from which judges derive and develop their concepts is the stock of decisions given by local tribunals. But here again, no individual decision as such defines the law for any other judge. Local decisions, however, again point out trends and directions, and help to clarify jurisprudential thinking. Hence, no one judge is bound by the decision of any other; but he (or she) would be wasting a resource of considerable value if they did not consult with the opinions and decisions of others.

It is a matter of record, as we have seen, that the grounds for nullity referred to as the *lack of due discretion* and *inability to assume the obligations of marriage* did not exist in the 1917 Code. However, on the basis of developing a natural law of concept (i.e. a person must be able to make a critical judgement concerning this marriage; and the person must be able to assume the obligations of marriage – otherwise the union would be invalid) Rotal and local jurisprudence has explored these concepts, and were finding marriages to be null and void on the strength of them throughout the 1940s and up to the 1980s; and it was this carefully worked out set of concepts which gave rise to the grounds being stated in the Code (can.1095 nn 2, 3). Therefore this second element of a nullity case is every bit as vital as the first.

The third essential element of a nullity case is the procedure. This is, as it were, the framework within which the other two elements exist. The rules of procedure for any nullity case are outlined in the Code of Canon Law. However, a word of explanation is called for here. The rules of procedure are given in Book VII of the Code. A brief glance at these rules, or the bulk of them, will indicate that the Church has in mind here a whole variety of kinds of case; not merely marriage nullity cases. The Church's Courts, from diocesan ones all the way to the Roman Rota and the Segnatura Apostolica, are geared to deal with cases such as libel, defamation, criminal matters, etc. This is the reason why the first part of Book VII concerns *Trials in General*, then *Contentious Trials*, and tacked on to the end of that section are certain specifics for marriage cases, penal cases and administrative procedures.

Hence, the procedure for a marriage nullity case takes elements from both the *Trials in General* section; as well as from the section on *Contentious Trials*; together with the specifics in marriage cases given between cann.1671 and 1707. Something of a similar kind existed in the 1917 Code (which came into operation on Whit Sunday in 1918) but then some 18 years later a special Instruction was produced in 1936 which gave the whole procedure culled from all parts of the Code for marriage cases in particular. This special Instruction was called (after the first three words of the document) *Provida Mater Ecclesia*. This was then partially modified by another post-conciliar document *Causas Matrimoniales* of 1971. A large number of the provisions of the latter document have been included in the present Code. However, no equivalent of *Provida* has been issued by the Holy See. This means that where the provisions of *Provida* are not in opposition to the present Code, it acts as a useful guide to procedure; but any new provisions in the present Code are, of course, not merely guidelines, but mandatory elements of the Church's Court procedure.

The Church's tribunals have existed for centuries. However, it is true to say that in the Middle Ages and after, such Courts relatively rarely dealt with marriage cases; marriages did not break down so frequently as they do today, and when they did break down, very few of them ever went before the Church's tribunals. The Church's Courts then were far more occupied with such matters as defamation or libel; cases of 'criminious clerks' (clergy) or 'renegade religious', as well as property and rights. The whole situation has become reversed in the present day: less than one percent of cases dealt with throughout the world are not cases relating to marriage in some way. Unless the Church has a special relationship with the civil authorities, there is no way in which cases other than those relating to conscience and the sacraments – as marriage cases – could ever be dealt with since ecclesiastical courts have no powers of compulsion. Hence, when the Church's Courts are referred to, it is almost always to do with marriage.

A further clarification may be made. Generally, each diocese has its own tribunal – at least in the western world. However, sometimes for the sake of convenience, a number of dioceses are grouped together to form a Regional Tribunal. What is said here will refer, with only a few differences, to both Diocesan and Regional Tribunals.

The Tribunal Personnel

The Diocesan Tribunal is part of the Bishop's Curia, that is his administration. The Tribunal deals with marriage cases, of which nullity cases generally form the bulk; but besides these there are also non-consummation and non-baptism cases. These last two kinds of cases will be examined in the next two chapters.

The Tribunal is presided over by an experienced Canon lawyer called the *Judicial Vicar*, also called under the earlier law the *Officialis*. He is responsible for arrangements being made for the interview of prospective clients; for applications for nullity to be dealt with in the Tribunal Office; for evidence to be taken; for personnel to be assigned to each case. He will be assisted by other priests, sisters and lay persons; and if the Tribunal is large enough and such help is needed, one of the assistants to the Judicial Vicar may be named the *Associate Judicial Vicar* (or *Vice-Officialis*). The Judicial Vicar has the same ordinary power in judicial matters as the Vicar General has in all other matters.

Whereas the term *Tribunal* in general covers the whole of the judicial organisation for dealing with marriage cases, the term *Court* is generally used to denote the specific set of persons designated to deal with an individual case. Since, of course, there will be a large number of cases being dealt with at any one time, each person will have been assigned to a number of different Courts; one Court per case. For each formal nullity case generally there would be a Court of some six persons designated.

To each case, in ordinary circumstances, three judges

would be assigned. The judges would be skilled in Canon law, and generally the Holy See expects the judges also to be qualified in Canon law, although it is permissible to seek from the Holy See special arrangements which would allow a judge who does not have formal qualifications in Canon law to act in a Tribunal provided he or she has adequate jurisprudential and procedural skills. Usually, the three judges do not actually sit together until the last stages of the case; and in the meanwhile, the Judicial Vicar or his Associate has supervised the preparation of the cases up to the stage of Decision by the judges. One of the three judges will be named as *Ponens*, the person who eventually leads the discussion of the case with the other two judges and then writes the *Sentence*, which gives the reasons in law and in fact for the decision that was given.

It should be noted here that there is a special provision which allows the Bishops' Conference to permit a local Bishop to entrust the case (and especially its Decision in the I Instance) to a sole clerical judge. This is by way of an exception because of the lack of suitably qualified judges. The Code also indicates that the sole judge can be assisted by two assessors or advisers who may be clerics or lay persons. In these circumstances the assessors are used as a sort of jury.

The Court will also have a *Defender of the Bond*. He or she will be a person skilled in Canon law whose role is to look after the interests of the bond of marriage. When someone petitions for a declaration of nullity, that person is alleging that the marriage is invalid. The Defender of the Bond's task is to monitor the process and to bring forward any arguments to show why the marriage should regarded as valid; or at least to show that the evidence is not strong enough for the judges to regard it as invalid. The petitioner can be represented by an *Advocate* whose role is to advance arguments on behalf of the petitioner to show why the marriage should be regarded as invalid. The Advocate and Defender of the Bond may be priests, sisters, or lay persons, provided they are adequately qualified.

Finally, each Court has a *Notary* who also can be a priest, sister or lay person. The Notary may take down the testimony at an evidence session, and is required to authenticate all documents as being originals or true copies. There is also an official called the *Promotor of Justice*. There can be situations in which it is not appropriate for either of the parties to an evidently invalid marriage to be the petitioner. If it becomes necessary for the public good to demonstrate the invalidity of such a case the Promotor of Justice takes over the role of alleging the invalidity, and acting in all respects as the petitioner: however the need for a Promotor of Justice to intervene is rare.

When a Tribunal has a large volume of business, it will be necessary to have a considerable back-up organisation for its efficient operation. This organisation will usually be provided by law persons, with the customary modern day office technology.

The Procedure

It is proposed to see what happens in a Tribunal from the time the first enquiry is made until the eventual decree of nullity is granted or refused. A case can be initiated in a number of different ways. The person may reach the Tribunal through a recommendation of his local priest; or through a counselling agency; even by making an enquiry of a national newspaper or one of the large number of women's magazines or an agony column; or sometimes by word of mouth of a friend, lawyer or doctor. When a person first gets in touch with a Tribunal, an appointment will be made for an interview. Usually most Tribunals, when making an appointment, ask the person to provide a certain amount of basic information – names, dates, places – and even an account of the marriage, its course and its breakdown. So far as the Church is concerned, anyone Catholic, non-Catholic, or even unbaptised, may petition a Tribunal for a case to be examined.

Mention must be made here of divorce. Before a person

can discuss the matter of nullity with a Tribunal, there must be clear evidence that the marriage has broken down. The way in which this is ensured (in countries where divorce exists) is to require anyone coming to a Tribunal to have a divorce decree absolute. The Church's attitude to divorce in a particular case is neutral. It regards divorce as a statement that a marriage has *de facto* broken down; and that all the necessary arrangements have been made to ensure the moral and economic welfare of the children and the parties themselves. The Church does not regard divorce as a permit to remarry. The need for a divorce to have been obtained before a marriage case can be started arises from the necessity to ensure that the marriage has broken down and that any concomitant civil litigation has been concluded. No Tribunal ever wants to be involved in civil divorce proceedings, or to be under *sub-poena* to give evidence or to asked for documents relating to a nullity case.

Diocesan Tribunals

When an appointment has been made for a person to visit a Tribunal, different practices are adopted by different Tribunals. But in general, the person will be seen by a Canon lawyer and the case would be discussed. At the interview it may emerge quickly that there is indeed a case and that there will be supporting evidence that is, witnesses. If this is the situation, a petition is drawn up and the various requirements for commencing a case are dealt with. There are usually certain forms to be completed and some formalities to be observed. But eventually the person would be sent a petition to study, correct and sign; together with other details such as checking witness details, addresses, and the like. When a person puts forward the names of witnesses, it must be understood that the witness has been asked by the petitioner to give evidence; and also details are required as to whether the witnesses will come to the Tribunal to give evidence or must be seen locally.

A case can go very wrong when a witness has been named and that witness has not been approached in advance by the petitioner. At the same time, the petitioner must be careful that the request for the witness to give evidence is made in very general terms, with no question of seeking to brief the witness as to what to say. If there is the slightest suspicion of a witness being briefed, the accusation of 'collusion' could well be brought by the Court or by the Defender of the Bond. This would inevitably react badly on the case.

When the petition has been signed (and names of the witnesses supplied) it is put formally to the Tribunal. The Presiding Judge appointed to deal with the case will examine the petition and determine whether it can be accepted for hearing or not. The petition must indicate:

- The judge to whom the case is directed (this would be the diocesan Bishop who is a judge in his own right).
- The grounds on which the invalidity is alleged, together with an indication of how the allegation is to be proved.
- The names and addresses of the petitioner and the respondent.
- The date; and the petition must, of course, be signed by the petitioner.

The Presiding Judge must (at least within a month) have decided whether he (the Court) is *competent* to deal with the case, whether the petition has satisfied the basic requirements mentioned above, and whether the case has a foundation. If the Presiding Judge is satisfied about these points, he formally accepts the petition; otherwise he formally rejects it. If it is rejected for some reason that can be corrected at once, the petitioner may re-draw the petition and submit it again. If the petition is rejected on the basis that there is no foundation to the case, the petitioner has the right to an appeal against this rejection. This appeal may either be made to the three judges in the case (if only the Presiding Judge by himself has rejected it) or to the Appeal Court of the Tribunal to which the petition was addressed (this is also called the II Instance Court).

Two issues need to be explained here. Firstly the term 'competence' which was mentioned above. Competence is the legal term given to a Court's ability to take and hear a case. A Tribunal is competent to deal with a case if it is the Tribunal of the diocese in which the marriage was celebrated; or if it is the Tribunal of the diocese in which the other party (the respondent) has a domicile or quasi-domicile. A Tribunal is also competent to hear a case if it is the diocese in which the petitioner is domiciled, provided that the petitioner and respondent live within the territory of the same Episcopal Conference; and this also requires the consent of the Judicial Vicar of the domicile of the respondent, (the Judicial Vicar already having consulted the respondent). Finally, a Tribunal is also competent if it happens to be the place where most of the evidence is to be collected, provided the Judicial Vicar of the respondent has given his permission; and the Judicial Vicar must also have asked the respondent if he has any objection. The *Segnatura Apostolica* lays out special provisions to be observed in the matter of competence.

The other point in connection with the acceptance or rejection of a petition concerns whether the petition has a foundation in law and fact; that is to say, whether it has enough substance. A petition may be submitted which has grounds alleged, good evidence available, and if all is proved clearly the marriage would be invalid. Of course, such a petition is accepted for hearing. However, a petition may adduce grounds, which if proved would clearly show that the marriage was null and void; but the petition or supporting documents indicate no way in which the grounds can be established; that is, there will be no proof. A Tribunal cannot accept a case which it knows in advance the petitioner cannot establish. On the other hand, the petition may state a whole series of facts and indicate how all these facts may be proved point by point;

but none of what is alleged would amount to nullity. Again, such a petition would be regarded as lacking any basis in law; and would have to be rejected. An appeal is possible for the petitioner, as already mentioned

When a petition has been accepted for trial, the next requirement is that the other party – the respondent – should be informed of the ensuing proceedings. The technical term for this phase is the *citation*. Normally this takes the form of a letter to the respondent advising him that his former partner has petitioned for the examination of the marriage and that the union has been alleged to be invalid on certain grounds. The respondent is also advised that there will be a meeting to be held in the future; and the grounds will be established for the alleged invalidity. He is also asked to indicate whether he would like to intervene in the proceedings, and whether he would like to give evidence; or he could choose to leave the whole matter to the Tribunal itself.

A reasonable length of time must be allowed for the respondent to reply. Often, the reply will be in the form of a document signed by the respondent indicating either that he wishes to take part in the proceedings or that he would prefer to leave the matter to the Tribunal. If there is no reply after a reasonable length of time, another letter may be sent. If it is clear that the respondent has received the letters and has not replied, then the proceedings can commence with a note entered into the documents of the case stating that the respondent has been cited, and that so far as can be ascertained he has received the citation, but he has not replied.

It can also happen that the petitioner has lost all track of the respondent. Steps may have to be taken to try to trace the respondent. Various means are employed by different Tribunals. For example, some advertise in the local press in the locality where the respondent was last known; others make use of the help offered by the Salvation Army to trace missing spouses; another way, more frequently used these days, is to request the Department of Social Security

(DSS) to pass on a letter. The DSS makes a search of its records and if there is a trace of the respondent, the letter will be passed on. A small charge is made. This method of endeavouring to trace the other party sometimes works; but because of remarriage, it is not so often successful in tracing female respondents.

When the respondent has indicated that he will co-operate or that he will leave the matter to the Court (or when he cannot be traced), the judge in charge of the case determines from the petition what precisely the grounds are to be and then formalises these grounds by means of a document, for example, 'the point at issue in this case was determined to be: total simulation on the part of the respondent husband'. When this has been done, evidence will be taken of the petitioner, the respondent and the witnesses. All these might visit the Tribunal (though never on the same occasion, so they do not meet) and give evidence at the Tribunal premises. Sometimes evidence has to be taken where the witnesses live, for example Halifax or Hong Kong. When the witness is located outside the diocese, the Tribunal requests that the Tribunal of the place of residence of the witness secures the evidence.

Generally questions are prepared (in advance) at the direction of the Presiding Judge. He has the responsibility of seeking and obtaining the truth. The Defender (and even the Advocate) may also submit questions to be put to the parties or witnesses. The questioning is carried out by the judge in the case; or evidence can also be taken by another person called an *Auditor* (see page 140).

Present at an evidence session will be the witness and the Auditor. Also present may be the Defender of the Bond and the Advocate, as well as a Notary. The witness is asked to take an oath of truthfulness before testifying. The manner in which the testimony is taken varies. It may be taken down by hand verbatim, or dictated on tape. Essentially, however, the witness must have the opportunity to hear or read what he has said and to change any part of the testimony. Eventually the evidence is agreed and signed by the witness and the auditor or the judge who takes the evidence, as well as by any other persons present.

The evidence session at the Tribunal is in no way comparable to a civil court's proceedings. The essence of a civil court is confrontation between the lawyers for each side of the case. This is not so in canonical proceedings. The essence of the latter procedure is that the judge is the one there to elicit the information, the whole truth. It is not left to lawyers to ask questions. The nearest comparison to a Church tribunal is a Coroner's court, in which the Coroner himself is charged with obtaining the truth from the witnesses (although there may be legal representation present for the various interested parties; but that is usually with a view to subsequent civil court proceedings). The Coroner's court is in fact the last relic of the old ecclesiastical procedure in England and Wales.

The Auditor or judge conducting the evidence session is there to obtain the truth. That is why there is no embargo on 'hearsay' evidence (as there is in civil courts). Hearsay evidence can be an extremely important source of information. However, the judge or auditor must ensure that the source of the hearsay evidence is carefully noted down. The three judges, when deciding the case at the end, have the task of weighing and evaluating the evidence and particularly hearsay evidence, and determining whether it is worthy of credence or not.

In questioning the witnesses, the Auditor must ensure that the questions are brief and simple; they must not be captious or deceptive; they must not be leading questions; and above all, the auditor must not harass or confuse the witness.

The witness is told at the end of the evidence session that the proceedings, and what has been said, are confidential, and is asked to undertake not to discuss the matter outside with others until the end of the case. When the witness has finished and departed, the auditor is required to write a short piece in which he gives his or her impressions about the witness: the certainty or otherwise with which he answered the questions; his grasp of facts and dates; the extent of his knowledge of the parties (a witness and not a principal); and the apparent truthfulness and reliability of the one testifying.

The session with a petitioner or respondent may have lasted, in a complicated matter, some three or four hours. Indeed sometimes it might be necessary for the petitioner to come back again for a further session to complete the testimony. Since the petitioner appreciates that this is for his own good, there is rarely any objection to this. For the other witnesses, the evidence sessions are usually shorter. However, the judges find that to hurry these sessions is useless, since the difficulty for a person searching his recollections, sometimes of events which took place a long time ago, is immense. Attempting to hurry the witness is self-defeating.

Depending upon the complexity of the case, there may be as many as six or more witnesses to be heard. Frequently, some of the witnesses live a long way from the Tribunal; sometimes they live abroad. It is usually quite easy to obtain their testimony. A request is sent to the dioceses where the other witnesses live. The local Tribunals take the required testimony with the same formalities as mentioned above. The testimony thus taken is returned to the Court and included in the dossier of the case. In this way it is possible to obtain evidence from place as far apart as South America or Australia, and even from otherwise inaccessible places like Iceland or Nepal. Wherever the Church has a Tribunal, it is possible to obtain the required testimony.

When all the evidence has been taken and transcribed, it will generally be examined carefully by an official of the Court to see what else needs to be done before the case moves to the next stage. This may involve the re-questioning of witnesses or of the principal parties; it may involve obtaining new witnesses; or a psychiatric report; or a psychological assessment on the party or parties; or upon the recorded evidence.

At this stage either party may wish to add further information. When the respondent has indicated that he has no interest in the case, this point hardly concerns him. But in any event, at the request of either party more evidence may be added to the case. At this stage also, relevant portions of the evidence may be shown, or better, explained, to the parties. But in these circumstances the Advocate for one (or one for each) party is most helpful in preserving the natural rights for each party.

When both the Defender and the Advocate are satisfied that all the possible relevant testimony has been obtained, the Presiding Judge then declares the evidence-collecting stage of the case to be concluded. At this point, the Advocate is requested to prepare his pleadings, showing why, from the evidence, the marriage in question should be regarded as null and void. He is given a certain length of time to write his observations, and within this time he must pass them back to the Presiding Judge. A copy of the pleadings is also supplied to the Defender of the Bond who then prepares his reply to the Advocate. The Defender shows, again from the evidence, why the marriage should be regarded as valid; or why the proper procedure has not been observed. The Advocate and the Defender have the opportunity of writing two (and sometimes in very complicated cases, three) sets of comments. Thereafter, the Presiding Judge declares this stage concluded.

Copies of all the evidence, documents and submissions of Advocate and Defender are then handed to the three judges in the case. A certain length of time is given for the judges to study the material, and a date is set for them to meet and discuss the case. Before the meeting, however, each of the judges has independently read the material, and reached his own conclusion on the case, and he comes to the meeting with a few pages of reasons showing why he has reached his decision. At this meeting, called the *Decisio*, the Ponens expounds the facts of the case and the judges discuss their own views. It is open to the judges to change their minds during the meeting, but when the discussion is concluded there is a vote and the result of the case rests upon a majority decision. The formula of the decision will be expressed thus: 'It appears proved (not proved) that the marriage in question is null and void on the grounds of [an intention against the permanence of marriage on the part of the respondent]'.

Where there is a negative decision, it will be noticed that the judges make no comment on the validity of the marriage as such. The decision merely states that 'it appears to be unproved'. Thus, when a negative decision is given against the petition, the judges are merely stating that the petitioner has not proved the invalidity. This is an important point, since it is always possible that the judges may have concluded that there is insufficient evidence to establish the nullity, whereas had there been more evidence, the marriage might well have been shown to be null and void. Hence, any comment on the validity of a marriage is carefully avoided.

The outcome of the meeting is advised to the petitioner, to his Advocate, to the Defender and to the respondent. It is then the obligation of the Ponens to write the Sentence. The Sentence is a series of reasons in law and in fact showing why and how the judges arrived at their decision. It sets out briefly a short synopsis of the case; then it gives the relevant points of law as they apply to the case in hand; and finally, there follows a series of arguments of the law applied to the alleged facts, showing the reasons for the decision.

The Appeal Court

If the decision is in favour of the petition – that is the judges in the I Instance Court have decided that the marriage in question appears to be null and void – the case must then be sent to its Appeal Court. At this stage it should be mentioned that when the judges vote on the case, and there is one judge who disagrees with the other two, he is allowed to write a 'dissenting judgement'. This will explain why his views are different from those of his colleagues. This dissenting judgement is also sent with the case on appeal.

When the case arrives at the Appeal Court, the first step is for the Appeal Court Defender of the Bond assigned to the case to read it; and to determine whether he would concur with the I Instance decision or not. If he agrees, then he passes the case back to the Appeal Tribunal stating that he has no objection to the decision being ratified by the Appeal Court; or, on the other hand, he may conclude in the reverse, and say that he would *not* wish the decision to be ratified.

The case then goes before the three judges of the Appeal Court. Independently, they study the case and each decides whether he would agree with the I Instance decision (taking into account the views of the II Instance Defender of the Bond). If the judges agree with the Instance decision by a majority vote, they then formally 'ratify' the I Instance decision; and accordingly the Appeal Court issues a decree of nullity. If the judges do not agree with the I Instance decision, they direct that the case be dealt with by means of the 'Ordinary Procedure' on appeal; with this direction go the reasons why the case could not be ratified – for example, more evidence might be required of the petitioner or the respondent; clarifications may be needed and so on.

If this is the situation, then the case proceeds along the same lines as at I Instance, that is with a citation to the respondent, and further evidence may be taken. When all that was required has been completed, the judges meet again (having had a further comment from the Defender of the Bond and more likely a further set of pleadings from the Advocate), they discuss and finally decide the case. Whatever their decision the Ponens writes up the Sentence; and if the decision was in favour of invalidity a decree of nullity is issued.

For a decree of nullity to be issued, it is already clear that there must be two *concordant* or agreeing decisions in favour of the petition. If one decision is affirmative and the other is negative, before a decree can be issued the case must be examined by a third Court. An appeal from a negative decision given in I Instance is dealt with according to the ordinary procedure. Below we will deal with the Roman Rota, which often plays the part of a III Instance Court. But there are other means by which a case can receive a third hearing without reference to the Rota. These will also be mentioned shortly.

Restrictive Clauses

It will be evident from some of the grounds of nullity already indicated that where a case is proved and the grounds reside in the petitioner, it may be necessary to exercise some caution about this petitioner marrying again. For example, if a non-Catholic petitioner alleged that he had an intention against the permanence of marriage when entering his first union; and this intention *contra bonum sacramenti*, as it is called, was proved to have existed. It is a matter of ordinary prudence to make quite certain that when this person marries again, this time in the Catholic Church, he does not have an intention of a similar nature. Consequently, to make quite sure that his intentions are proper, this time, it is not unusual for the Appeal Court to add a *restrictive clause* to the decree of nullity.

The purpose of this restrictive clause is to put up a signal (which is recorded with the person's baptismal register entry) that special care should be taken in the preparation for this new marriage. This would generally mean that the priest who is involved in the preparation for the new marriage would have to ensure that the person's intentions with regard to permanence are now in accordance with the requirements of the Church. The same thing, of course, refers to all grounds alleged in nullity cases. It is important to ensure that the second union is not affected by the same ground of nullity as existed at the time of the first union. Often, a Bishop establishes a special office to deal with such situations.

However, it should also be repeated that no local Bishop can establish a diriment impediment to marriage; that is to say, he cannot prevent this particular marriage from taking place under pain of nullity, unless he is *morally certain* that the forthcoming union would be invalid. Clearly, this is no easy matter, indeed it is questionable whether such a conclusion could ever be possible. But essentially the restrictive clause needs to be seen as a 'marker' that special care should be taken over any further union.

The above account is a very brief outline of the formal nullity procedure. It will be clear from this that certain basic elements underline the procedure. We have already mentioned the matter of the type or nature of the process, that it is not like an English civil law process, but essentially a documentary and closed procedure. There are a number of further points, however, which must now be mentioned.

The Burden of Proof

In any legal process there are certain assumptions upon which the Court must work. For example, in civil law, there is a presumption that the ordinary man knows what he is doing when he performs some action. It is not *assumed* that the person concerned is mentally unbalanced; this must be proved. Again, when a person buys a suite of furniture, it is assumed that he actually intends to do this. Subsequently, he may seek to prove that at the time he was not mentally competent or that some other fact would mean the contract was invalid. In Canon law, it is assumed that when a person says the words and performs certain actions at the altar during a wedding ceremony, he intends to convey by these means that he intends to be married. Thus, when a person has made the answers and indicated his consent to the marriage, he is presumed to have intended to marry; and he is presumed to be validly married.

If, subsequently, he or his partner wishes to impugn the validity of the marriage – for example, to assert that the man did not have the intention to contract marriage at all – then it would be for the person making this allegation to prove it. This is obvious and reasonable. Hence, when we speak of the burden of proof in connection with a nullity case, we mean that the onus of establishing that the marriage is invalid, that the person did not intend to contract the marriage, rests on the person alleging this – that is, the petitioner. It follows from this that the petitioner must bring forward such evidence as will upset the presumption that the man concerned intended to contract a proper marriage. In other words, there is a presumption that a marriage is valid, which remains until this presumption is upset. This is the task of the petitioner. When a petitioner is not successful in bringing forward sufficient evidence to upset the presumption of validity, the judges must return a decision of *non constat de nullitate* or 'it does not appear that the marriage in question is invalid'.

The Rejection of the Petition

We have already mentioned that there is a stage, just after the appointment of the Court, when the petition submitted is examined and if it does not conform to the rules of competence or it does not have some substance as a case, it is rejected. That is to say that the Court rules that the petition cannot be accepted for trial. When rejecting a petition, the Court must give reasons for the rejection. As has been said, there are two principal reasons for rejection: one relating to competence, and the other relating to the lack of substance (or at least that the petition does not state adequately the substance, which may well exist). If the rejection is on the grounds that the Tribunal is not competent to deal with the case, the petitioner must be advised of this, and also told which would be the competent Tribunal to which the petition should be submitted.

On the other hand, if the petition is not evidently based upon adequate *grounds* for nullity, this must be indicated to the petitioner. It may happen that the petition had been badly drawn up and that it does not express what is in the petitioner's mind, in which case it maybe possible for the petition to be altered so as to provide further details which would make it acceptable to the Court.

It can also happen that the Court rejects the petition on the basis that there is insufficient substance to the case – that is to say that even if proved, the grounds alleged would not indicate the nullity of marriage, or else that the grounds alleged are patently false. A Court might also reject a petition if it is quite clear that though there are grounds of nullity, it is evidently impossible to establish these grounds through necessary evidence. In any event, if the petition is rejected and it cannot be altered by the petitioner, the latter has the right to appeal against the rejection.

There are two ways in which an appeal against the rejection of a petition can be made. If the original petition was rejected by a Presiding Judge acting alone, then the appeal is to the College of three judges appointed to the case. On the other hand, if the rejection was made by one judge who was the only judge appointed to deal with the case, or if the original rejection was made by the three judges acting in a collegiate fashion appointed to the case, the appeal is then to the II Instance Court.

The Roman Rota

It will be clear from the account of the nullity process already given that in normal circumstances the Roman Rota is not involved in ordinary diocesan trial of marriage cases. But there are situations in which the Rota may be involved. We have already mentioned the necessity of there being two affirmative decisions before a decree of nullity can be issued. Where the petitioner has received one affirmative and one negative decision, a third hearing is required. The case can be sent to the Roman Rota to be dealt with in the III Instance. An affirmative decision given there would then mean that a decree of nullity can be issued. However, it is not always necessary to go to the Rota for a third hearing of a case. The Holy See does give permission, though on an *ad hoc* basis, for a third hearing to take place in some local diocese. The advantage of a III Instance hearing being dealt with locally is speed. The Rota has a large number of cases, and the procedure there is consequently slower than when a case is dealt with locally. However, permission for a III Instance hearing to take place locally is not automatically granted by the Holy See (that is, by the Segnatura Apostolica).

Another situation in which a case might be referred to the Rota is when a petitioner, having received a negative decision in Ist Instance, wishes to appeal directly to the Holy See. This he is permitted to do by referring to the Rota; but it then means that if the second decision is affirmative, the III Instance hearing must also be dealt with at the Rota (with a separate panel of judges). Moreover, for very special reasons, a person may request to have his case dealt with from the very beginning by the Roman Rota. This may happen when, for instance, the petitioner is very well known in his own diocese and by the members of the Tribunal. He can be given permission to start his case from the beginning with Roman Rota.

Time and Expense

It will be noticed that the procedures described, because of the great care that must be taken with the processing of a nullity case, must involve a very considerable amount of time The actual time taken in the treatment of a case depends largely on the Tribunal concerned. Obviously, where the Tribunal is small, where there are not many cases, the personnel will be relatively inexperienced in the actual processing of the cases that do come before them. This could mean considerable delay. On the other hand, where there is a much larger Tribunal dealing with a much larger volume of cases, though the processing of a case may take a shorter time, the expenses will be, for that very reason, the heavier. It is clear that the time factor or the expenses involved cannot be analysed here since these depend largely on the Tribunal concerned. The petitioner would be wise to obtain an idea of how long the case will take by asking the officials of the Tribunal, where also some indication of the expenses involved will be discovered.

In any event, it is now almost standard practice for a Tribunal to seek a deposit against the expenses of the future work on the case. The amount of the deposit, of course, varies depending upon the Tribunal. However, it must also be said that no case is ever refused because of a person's lack of funds. If need be the case is dealt with entirely on the basis of the Church's free legal aid. In this case the expenses are defrayed by the offerings of the faithful in their parish churches. The Church's 'free legal aid' system is the oldest in the world, dating from the early 17th century.

Delays in marriage nullity cases almost invariably arise because of the length of time taken in obtaining evidence. It will be appreciated that when all the evidence can be taken at the Tribunal Offices (the parties and the witnesses attending the evidence sessions by appointment), evidence can be gathered fairly speedily. The delays occur when a request for evidence has to be sent elsewhere. This can either be within the diocese in question; or elsewhere in the country; or abroad.

One way in which the problem of delays in evidence taking is being tackled around the world is to recruit a body of lay volunteers to assist in the process. Such volunteers are carefully selected specially from among persons recently retired; or professional persons who have more time at their disposal; housewives whose children are at school; sisters from religious congregations and parish sisters, and so on. Such volunteers are generally given a short course on the skills of evidence taking; and they often sit in once or twice with another experienced evidence taker (Auditor); and then start their own work.

These Lay Auditors are specially 'commissioned' (rather in the manner of special Ministers for the Eucharist), and given refresher courses or in-service training as they continue their work. It has been generally found that this system has worked well. The standard of evidence taking is very high, and the delays have been dramatically reduced. This work is seen by the lay auditors as a way in which they are able to bring their own special skills to contribute to the pastoral as well as the judicial activity of the Church.

The Informal or Administrative Procedure

We have already indicated that there is one procedure for the treatment of nullity cases which involve some sort of defect of consent. This same procedure is also used for the proof of certain diriment marriage impediments. However, there are other impediments, though nonetheless causing the nullity of marriage, which can be established by means of an informal or administrative procedure. This informal procedure requires that the impediment is able to be established by means of *certain* and *authentic* documents. If such documents can be produced, together with the citations mentioned in connection with the formal procedure, and the inspection of the documents by the Defender of the Bond, such a marriage can be declared and null and void without further ado. To illustrate the working of this procedure, we give below a short case illustrating the procedure in a case for the impediment of previous marriage, or ligamen together with what information must be obtained to demonstrate the nullity of the marriage. Before turning to the example, however, we must recall that the informal process can be used for establishing at least the following impediments: disparity of cult, solemn vow of chastity, the bond of sacred orders, previous marriage, consanguinity, affinity and spiritual relationship.

Peter and Doreen (ligamen)

Peter Smith spoke to his parish priest about marrying **Doreen**, who was previously married. He told the priest that since Doreen had been married in the Register Office, he had always assumed that this was an invalid marriage, and that, therefore, at some time he would be able to marry her. The priest warned Peter that, assuming Doreen is not a Catholic, and assuming that Doreen's former husband was also not a Catholic, her first marriage was probably valid. However, the priest said that he would go into the case. The priest saw Doreen and discovered that neither she nor her husband were Catholic. But he did learn that her former husband had himself previously married and divorced. The priest, thereupon, had good reason to refer Peter and Doreen to the Tribunal.

When Doreen was interviewed at the Tribunal, the following story emerged. Doreen had been married to **James** on 14 April 1961, but James had left Doreen for another woman, and Doreen had divorced James. The decree of divorce was made out to 19 March 1966. Doreen knew that James had been previously married, but she did not know much about that union; and nothing about the former wife other than that James had always called her an agnostic. James had divorced her on the grounds of adultery. Doreen did not have anything else to tell the Tribunal.

The Judicial Vicar asked Doreen to obtain from the General Register Office a copy of her marriage certificate relating to the union with James. This certificate showed that James had been formerly married. Therefore, a search was made for certificates relating to a marriage and a *divorce in James's name prior to April 1961. After some searching the documents were discovered. They showed that James had married **Sandra** on 18 November 1956, and that James was described as single at the time, as also was Sandra. A divorce decree which was also found showed that this same union had been dissolved and the decree had been made absolute on 16 July 1960. The Judicial Vicar also asked Doreen to make a further search for a marriage certificate in the name of Sandra (with her own original maiden name or with James's surname) for some time after July 1960. Such a certificate was found, and it showed that Sandra had been remarried on 24 July 1961 to a man called **Cyril**. Finally, the Judicial Vicar asked Doreen to find out something about the religion of James and Sandra. Doreen knew James's mother, and the latter was able to state that James had been baptised in the Church of England in a village in Norfolk. From there, Doreen obtained a copy of James's baptismal certificate. James's mother also knew that Sandra was an unbeliever, and that her parents had also been unbelievers. She knew that Sandra's mother had originally been a member, though not a practising one, of the Presbyterian Church, but Sandra had never been raised in any religion at all.*

When all this information had been collected the Judicial Vicar made a list of all the documents he had obtained and alongside each document he showed what the document established. The following are the documents which were produced:

1 *Marriage Certificate of James and Sandra, married on 18th November 1956 at Chiswick Register Office.*

2 *Divorce Decree Absolute for the same union; made absolute on 16 July 1960.*

3 *Baptismal Certificate of James (Church of England), and testimony of James's mother that he always belonged to the Church of England.*

4 *Information from James's mother – given on oath – that Sandra had been the child of non-Catholic parents; and had been brought up with no religion.*

5 *Marriage Certificate of Sandra and Cyril, married on 24 July 1961 at Chelsea Register Office.*

6 *Marriage Certificate of James and Doreen, married on 14th April, 1961 at the Paddington Register Office.*

7 *Divorce Decree Absolute for the same union (No. 6 above) dated 19 March 1966.*

With all this information the Judicial Vicar could make out a statement to the effect that when James had married Doreen he was already (in terms of Canon law) married to Sandra. To all intents and purposes the union with Sandra had been valid – neither were bound to the form of marriage (since neither were Catholics), and both were at the time of this first union single persons. Furthermore, when James married Doreen, Sandra was still alive (as shown by the fact that she contracted a marriage after the date of Doreen's marriage to James). Hence, when all the documents had been produced, and James had been cited (advised that his marriage to Doreen was undergoing scrutiny with a view to an ecclesiastical declaration of nullity and told the reasons), the Defender of the Bond was able to examine the papers and to state that all the documents were in order. Thereafter, the Judicial Vicar signed a declaration of nullity.

This is a short example of the informal process for nullity, which, together with the other, formal process, is used by the Church either when it is alleged that there was something wrong with the consent of one of the parties, or when there was an alleged undispensed diriment impediment preventing a couple from marrying validly. We now leave our consideration of the nullity of marriage and turn to the Church's procedure for dispensing a marriage which had not been consummated.

Section IV

UNCONSUMMATED MARRIAGE

Chapter Eight

DISPENSING AN UNCONSUMMATED UNION

W E HAVE already said that according to the teaching of the Church a marriage that is valid, sacramental and consummated cannot be set aside by any human power. Such a union is regarded as indissoluble, binding until the death of one of the spouses. In the preceding chapters we have examined the situation if it is alleged that a marriage is not valid. In this chapter we look at the situation, and the possibilities, if the marriage is alleged to be unconsummated. First of all it should be said that the teaching that the Pope has the power to dispense a marriage which has never been consummated goes back to the Middle Ages. There was considerable discussion amongst theologians and lawyers concerning precisely what constituted marriage. It will be appreciated that the view which maintained that the marriage was made through consummation also implied that until consummation had taken place the marriage had not yet fully come into being. On the other hand, the view which maintained that consent made the marriage, did not disregard the element of consummation altogether. It did not regard consummation as being the constitutive element of marriage, though without consummation it was not considered a complete marriage.

Apart from the historical aspect of the matter, it is quite clear when speaking of marriage as a union in which the parties pledge to each other the rights over their bodies, where consummation does not take place, there is something missing from the fulfilment of this pledge. When a couple marry validly, but agree that they will not make use of their marital rights, this very statement indicates that they do appreciate that they have exchanged these marital rights. However, when a couple do choose to exercise their marital rights, but for some reason, other than their own joint wills, this exercise cannot take place, then there is something deficient in their marriage. When this deficiency is caused by the will of one of the parties, obviously the other party is gravely wronged, even on the basis of a natural contract, let alone on the basis of a sacramental union. Thus when a marriage has not been consummated (unless it is by the express and free agreement of both parties), then there is something gravely amiss with the union. It is this type of union with which we will now deal.

There are a few types of tribunal case which carry with them the pain and suffering involved in a marriage that has failed through the tension arising from sexual troubles between a couple. Since the sexual life of the parties is a normal and holy part of marriage involving the participation with God in the possible formation of a new human being, and which is the normal and expected means through which a couple will show their love one for the other, the failure in this respect usually produces a state almost amounting to shock, certainly of frustration, sometimes of anger, and always a deep unhappiness on the part of at least one of the spouses. This is often an area of marriage in which the couple are too shy to seek advice. Often they merely hope and pray that something will happen so that all will come right. Unfortunately, because of this inclination to say little or to remain entirely silent about the problem, sometimes the trouble is allowed to persist too long.

A lot of the work of Marriage Counselling Agencies is centred in this area of marriage problems. But by the time the couple have referred to such organisations, it may be too late. The marriage may have broken down, or at very least the health of one or both of the parties may have suffered so considerably as a result of the problem that there is sometimes little else a couple can do but to separate. It is quite obvious, therefore, that wherever a problem such as this arises in a marriage – normally very soon after the marriage – help should be sought at once. The work of marriage tribunals is sad, since they so frequently have to deal with marriages that have already broken down for this reason.

It is frequently said, since the couple when they marry agree that they will pledge themselves to each other 'in sickness and in health', that merely because a couple have not been able to have intercourse, this is hardly a reason for separating. This is to misunderstand the nature of marriage, and to over-estimate the human condition. Where the couple have pledged themselves to each other for life, including the physical rights over their bodies, there is an assumption that normal intercourse will be able to take place. This assumption is based on the whole notion of the mutual physical exchange. If it is not possible for this exchange to take place, there is obviously something missing from the union. Even though the condition in one of the parties may be the result of some sickness, nonetheless the words 'in sickness and in health' hardly refer to this type of sickness, which strikes at the whole basis of the marriage. It is for this reason that for certain special situations and upon certain conditions, the Pope sometimes grants a dispensation, which enables one or both parties to remarry.

In a non-consummation case put to the Holy Father, there are two elements that must be clearly established. One element is that the marriage has not in fact been consummated, and the other is that there are sufficiently good reasons why the dispensation should be granted. We will now deal with these two requirements.

Proof of Non-Consummation

To begin with, it is necessary that we re-state clearly what the Church understands by consummation. The definition of consummation already given is: the penetration of the vagina by the erect male member, and ejaculation within the vagina. We have already seen something of the present matter when dealing with the impediment of impotence. Obviously, for consummation to take place, the definition mentioned above must be fulfilled. Rather than deal here with physical conditions which prevent consummation, which would come under the heading of impotence, we will concentrate upon proof of the fact that the marriage has not been consummated. It is necessary to appreciate that wherever there exists a condition of absolute or relative impotence which is perpetual, and antecedent to the marriage, then obviously it is not possible to consummate the marriage. However, here we will deal with the situation, which all too frequently arises, where *separately*, all the elements of the definition above *seem* to be possible, but for some other reason the marriage is not consummated. For example, it might be possible for there to be proper and complete erection of the male member, and yet still be no consummation, in the canonical sense. Or though the male is capable of erection and ejaculation he may not be capable of penetration.

Frequently, medical specialists advise that there is no evident bar to consummation, and yet nonetheless it has not taken place. This can often be due to a lack of confidence on the part of the couple, or nervousness, or fear, with consequent tension preventing penetration. It is well to remember that, generally, non-consummation is the fault of neither spouse, and often with different partners consummation may be a matter of ease and simplicity. However, the task of the Matrimonial Tribunal is to collect the evidence and try to establish the facts.

Since the dispensation of marriage on the grounds of non-consummation is a power only exercised by the Holy Father himself, the first point to be stated here is that local Diocesan Tribunals act as agents for the Holy See. They do not act 'of their own proper competence', and the final decision in the case is taken in Rome, not by the local

Tribunal. When the dossier has been completed by the local Tribunal it is submitted to the Congregation of the Sacraments in Rome.

To begin a non-consummation case, it is necessary to assemble various documents and a petition. The documents are the baptismal and marriage certificates, and proof that the marriage has broken down, a civil divorce or nullity decree. With these documents the bishop is then able to appoint a Court to take the evidence in the case.

For this type of case the Court consists of an Instructing Judge, the Defender of the Bond, and a notary. The Instructing Judge arranges for the petitioner to give evidence. It is assumed, for the purposes of this description of the process, that the petitioner has already been examined by a doctor (who, it is hoped, may have been able to certify that the girl is *virgo intacta*). On the other hand it is not the situation that without such a medical report a case can never be sent to Rome. It depends on the case.

Since, as it will be appreciated, some of the evidence that must be taken is of a very personal nature, it is normal and appropriate that the interrogation of the wife be carried out by a doctor who would deal with the actual details of attempts at consummation and the like. This interrogation by the doctor may be carried out in a hospital or in the doctor's consulting rooms, or at the Tribunal. Besides the questions by the doctor, the petitioner is also asked by the Instructing Judge (on the same or some other occasion) questions on more general matters, for example, how she came to meet her husband, when they married, whether they were happy to begin with, how and when the marriage started to break down. Where possible the Instructing Judge would be accompanied by a notary. When all this evidence has been taken down, it is checked through by the petitioner and signed. There is also here an oath of secrecy to be taken by all the witnesses. The members of the court are already bound by their strict oath of office, and the doctor is in any case bound by his bond of professional confidence. Thereafter, the evidence of the other spouse is taken in a similar manner.

The very nature of this type of case is such that there can be no witnesses in the strict sense of the word. Indeed it will have been observed that this type of case goes through, apart from the evidence of the doctors, entirely upon the word and good standing and known honesty of the two parties to the case as verified by the witnesses. However, it will be seen that the term 'witness' covers two different kinds of person. There is one type of witness who states what he knows about consummation of the marriage. That is, he says what he has 'heard' about this. In this sense he is a hearsay witness, but provided that the evidence can be assessed as truthful and relevant, such hearsay witnesses can be valuable for the establishment of the truth. The other type of witness is a character witness. That is, since the case is based very much upon the truthfulness and good faith of the parties, it may be useful to have statements of witnesses who can vouch for the truthfulness and honesty of the parties. The Court will try to assemble, from the two parties, the names and addresses of both hearsay and character witnesses. We can show here by means of an example how the testimony of these two types of witness can be of assistance.

Robert and Sophie

*Let us call the petitioner **Sophie** and her husband **Robert**, They had met at their Teachers' Training College. They married in 1983, and although they attempted intercourse on many occasions, this was never successful. After about a year, during which time they had mentioned the trouble to no one, they realised they must seek professional help and they saw their general practitioner. He examined them both but he could find nothing physically wrong with either party. Thinking that the trouble might be psychological, he referred them to a Catholic psychiatrist. The latter realised that there was something radically wrong with Robert, and began treatment. In the meanwhile,*

*Sophie confided her troubles to her mother, who also mentioned the matter to her husband. The mother, feeling unable to be of any real assistance, also suggested that Sophie should speak to her older sister, who was happily married with four children. Sophie therefore, confided in the sister, **Veronica**.*

Unfortunately, the treatment that Robert received did not help, and indeed matters became steadily worse. The effect on the nerves of both Sophie and Robert was appalling. Finally the psychiatrist, realising that he could not help Robert, suggested that for the sake of the couple's health they might try a temporary separation. Being ready to try any remedy, the couple separated. They both still felt they were very much in love, but that the strain of the relationship was corroding their lives. When they did come together again, there was still no improvement. By this time the general practitioner was becoming alarmed about the effect on Sophie, and he consulted with the psychiatrist. They both thought that the only remedy to the sad situation was for the couple to separate again, with the option of returning to each other in three months. However, after three months had elapsed, Sophie was no better, and it was thought that permanent separation was the only solution. Both Sophie and Robert realised that there was no hope for them together, and so they finally parted in mid-1985.

Sophie slowly returned to health after her near nervous breakdown. Robert also recovered, but the couple could not go back to each other. Sophie approached the Tribunal to see whether the Holy Father would grant a dispensation, so that she could remarry and have children. Robert was also anxious to remarry and to have children too, and he readily agreed that this approach to the Holy Father was the proper course.

The Tribunal, having considered this a worthy petition, began a non-consummation case. Sophie gave evidence, being questioned about the intimate side of the married life by a Tribunal doctor. She had already been examined by one doctor, and his report said that Sophie was virgo intacta. Thereafter, Robert gave evidence to the Court. Meanwhile, the Tribunal compiled a list of those who could give evidence in the case. Firstly, there was the petitioner's mother and father, and the sister Veronica. Robert had also mentioned the matter to his father at the time that he first began to receive treatment from the psychiatrist. Two other witnesses were the general practitioner and the psychiatrist. The two doctors, being bound by their bond of professional confidence, could only answer questions for the Tribunal on condition that their respective patients had signed release notes. In addition to this, it was also possible for the Tribunal to obtain excellent character witnesses for both parties.

In an example like the case of Robert and Sophie, all three persons are asked to give 'evidence' to the Tribunal. The 'hearsay' witnesses are asked, amongst other things, when they were first told about the couple's marriage problem, whether this was before or after the separation, and any other relevant details they might know about. When all this material has been gathered, it is transcribed into four copies. One of these copies is passed to the Defender of the Bond who may have been present at some of the evidence sessions. He carefully examines all the evidence, and sees whether it contains any inherent contradictions. He sees to what extent the spouses are vouched for as honest and trustworthy, and makes certain that, so far as is possible, all the regulations of the Sacred Congregation of the Sacraments on this matter have been observed. Any observations that he has to make on either of these two counts he sets down in his 'comments' which he returns to the Tribunal.

The whole dossier together with the comments of the Defender of the Bond are then submitted to the Bishop. Often the Instructing Judge has been through all the material himself and made some comments for the assistance of the Bishop. In any event the Bishop prepares his 'opinion' on the case, making special mention of whether he regards the allegation of non-consummation as established, whether the petitioner is a worthy person, and whether he recommends the petitioner to the Holy Father. This 'opinion', together with three copies of the whole dossier, is then sent to the Congregation of the Sacraments in Rome.

At the Congregation, where the case is handled on behalf of the Holy Father, another Court is appointed. This time, the Court consists of a Defender of the Bond and three Commissioners. The Defender of the Bond examines the case, and writes his comments. He passes these to the Congregation, and the comments together with the whole dossier are then submitted to each of the three Commissioners. These priests carefully and independently examine all the material, and at some appointed time they meet and vote on the case. If the decision is in favour of the petition, that is, if they decide that the evidence has established the non-consummation and a dispensation should be granted, their recommendations are then submitted to the Cardinal Prefect of the Congregation. The latter personally takes a resumé of this case, together with many others, to the Holy Father and advises him of the opinion of the Sacred Congregation. If the Holy Father agrees, the Congregation then issues the necessary dispensation in the name of the Pope. In due course this decree will be sent to the local diocese, and the Instructing Judge will communicate the decision to the parties concerned. On receipt of the dispensation, provided there are no restrictive clauses inserted in the text, both parties are advised that they are now free to remarry. (see Appendix I for the norms issued by the Holy See for the conduct of such cases).

Having dealt with the procedure for handling a case, we must now consider a few further points, namely the merits of the petitioner, restrictive clauses and the time and expenses which necessarily become involved in a non-consummation case.

Merits of Petitioner

As we have already mentioned, since we are speaking of a valid and sacramental union, a dispensation of an unconsummated marriage is something granted by the Holy Father as a favour and not as a right. For this reason, the merits of the petitioner and the reasons for the petition will be carefully considered in deciding whether to grant the dispensation, once the non-consummation has been established. Firstly, under this heading it must be mentioned that the Holy See will not ordinarily accept a petition when there has been a history of contraception in the marriage. It will be appreciated that where use has been made of sheath contraceptives, and this was the only form of intercourse, it follows that according to the definition already given, consummation in the strict sense *may not* have taken place. In such circumstances, a person could technically seek to petition for a dispensation. However, the Holy See does not accept a petition where this has been the case. One reason is that since this is a favour granted where the couple *have not been able* to have intercourse, it would be too much of a fiction if the Holy See granted a dispensation where the contravention of the Church's law is made the basis of the petition. The other reason, equally important, is that since it is never certain, and obviously not capable of proof, that a sheath contraceptive is effective, it cannot be stated with certainty that there was no ejaculation in the vagina. Obviously in the case of other contraceptive devices, or of the pill, this latter point does not arise since the definition of consummation is either realised or it is not.

Besides this point, the Holy See always seeks a reason for granting a dispensation, even when it has been established with moral certainty that a marriage has not been consummated. Therefore, to petition the Holy See so as to contract another marriage where the person concerned has been the wilful cause of the breakdown of the first union (apart from the non-consummation, that is) would not be considered as a reason for granting the dispensation. However, since any one petitioning the Holy See for this favour obviously has a reason, normally to remarry within the Church, to have a family and to lead a normal Catholic Family life, this point is usually academic. It is merely mentioned here in order to stress that the granting of the dispensation does not automatically follow upon proof of non-consummation.

Restrictive Clauses

We have already looked at restrictive clauses as attached to decrees of nullity. Such clauses may also figure in non-consummation cases. Occasionally the reason for the non-consummation may be the antecendent and perpetual impotence of one of the parties. Or rather, it might be surmised that this is the reason. Or the reason may be that one of the parties was the deliberate and wilful cause of the non-consummation, that is, that the person concerned refused to consummate the marriage. When the Holy Father grants a dispensation, it means that the marriage in question is dissolved. Thus, at least technically, both parties are free to contract other marriages. It is for this reason that occasionally the Holy See attaches a restrictive clause to the dispensation. It might be stipulated, for example, that one of the parties is not permitted to remarry without the permission of the Bishop of the diocese, or that of the Sacred Congregation; or indeed that the other party is not permitted to marry at all. Such a restrictive clause is noted in the Baptismal Register as in the case of a nullity decree (see page 145).

Time and Expense

The same points about time and expense apply to non-consummation cases as to nullity cases. The expenses in this situation obviously include costs incurred in the case being sent to Rome; and the time taken will obviously have to reflect the fact that the matter must be dealt with in two separate places. However, enquiries to the local Tribunal will indicate what the time factor is likely to be.

In this chapter we have tried to describe the typical procedure for a non-consummation case. Naturally there will be considerable variation in the details depending upon who the petitioner is (husband or wife); whether both parties co-operate; whether there is adequate evidence of the facts alleged, and many other factors. Here we have merely outlined the simplest type of non-consummation case, and obviously this outline cannot cover all the possible combinations of circumstances. However, the description of the procedure will convey some idea of the work involved in such a case.

Section V

NON SACRAMENTAL MARRIAGE

Chapter Nine

THE PAULINE AND
PETRINE PRIVILEGES

W E HAVE already explained what the Church understands to be grounds for the invalidity of marriage, and also what is understood by the non-consummation of a union. Finally, we must deal with the situation when it is alleged that the marriage contracted is not a sacrament. When we speak of a marriage being non-sacramental, we have to bear in mind that the sacrament of marriage, like the other sacraments, can only be received by a person who is himself a Christian. Moreover since the sacrament of matrimony relates to two people, by making them one, it follows that for the one sacrament of marriage to be received by both parties, it is necessary that both of them have been baptised. When both parties are baptised, all other things being equal, this couple can confer on each other the sacrament of matrimony. We must now consider the situation when one of the parties to the marriage is not baptised.

That the Pope sets aside non-sacramental unions – for good reasons – can be established from the history of the Church. There have been countless examples of the Popes exercising this power. It is important, however, that this power of the Pope to set aside the union of a couple wherein one of the parties has not been baptised is carefully distinguished from the Pauline Privilege.

The Pauline Privilege

The Pauline Privilege is based on the text of the first letter of St Paul to the Corinthians (1 Cor 7:8-15). Here, the

Apostle is considered to have been speaking of the situation in which two pagans marry, and subsequently one of them receives the sacrament of baptism. Thereafter, the unbaptised party refuses to live peacefully with the Christian party, without 'offence to the Creator', and does not wish himself to be baptised. In such circumstances, these three conditions must be properly established:

- Baptism of only one party.
- Refusal to live peacefully.
- No conversion of the other party.

If they are, and the marriage has actually broken down, the Christian party is permitted by the Bishop of the place to proceed to a new marriage. It is held in such a case that the first marriage is dissolved by the 'exercise of the Pauline Privilege'.

In the procedure relating to the Pauline Privilege, it must be clearly established that the couple cannot live together. To ascertain this, the non-Christian party is to be questioned, or perhaps there may already be a divorce, which would demonstrate the couple's irreconcilability. Although this type of case is relatively simple, it used not to occur very frequently in western Europe. However, with fewer non-Catholics being baptised, and with the great influx of persons outside the Christian tradition from the Middle and Far East there are now many more such cases, both of the Pauline and the Petrine Privileges. In countries where Christian baptism is rare, the exercise of the Pauline Privilege is more frequent. Regardless of the frequency of the use of the Pauline Privilege, it will be noticed that this procedure differs considerably from the 'dissolution of the natural bond' to which we now turn.

The Petrine Privilege

In the dissolution of the natural bond, an extension of the Pauline Privilege called the Petrine Privilege, or dissolution 'in favour of the faith', it must be established that *one* of the parties to the original marriage was not baptised.

When this can be shown with certainty, it follows that the marriage in question was not a sacrament. Where this is the case, in certain circumstances a petition may be put to the Holy Father asking that the former union be dissolved 'in favour of the faith' of the Catholic party who is now involved.

The Holy See at present will accept a petition from an unbaptised person who now wishes to marry a Catholic; from a previously unbaptised person, now baptised as a non-Catholic, and who wishes to marry another Catholic; from a previously unbaptised person, now a Catholic, who wishes to marry another Catholic (or at least a baptised non-Catholic); and also from a Catholic previously married to an unbaptised person (with a dispensation from disparity of cult) who now wishes to marry another baptised person. However, currently the Holy See will not accept a request from a baptised petitioner, previously married to an unbaptised person, and who having been received into the Church, wishes to marry another unbaptised person.

When a person petitions the Holy Father for a dissolution of a marriage on the grounds that one of the parties to the union was not baptised, there are two basic requirements. Firstly, it must be established that the person concerned was not baptised at the time of the marriage and, if he was subsequently baptised, that the couple did not live together as man and wife after the baptism. Secondly, there must be adequate reasons why the Holy Father is asked to dissolve the union.

Proof of Non-Baptism

It is, of course, extremely difficult to prove that something did not happen – indeed it is a logical impossibility. This, to some extent, explains the reason why a natural bond case can involve some difficulty. However, in spite of the difficulties, it is possible to become *morally* certain that a baptism did not take place. The whole process concerning the natural bond of marriage is governed by a special Instruction of the Congregation for the Doctrine of the Faith, the new name for the Holy Office (See Appendix II). There are two basic features of this proof. The positive feature is that 'evidence' must be taken from persons who would have been in a position to know whether the child was baptised. For example, the child's parents, or close relatives such as aunts and uncles. It is necessary that whoever does give evidence should have known the person concerned in childhood. For example, it is hardly worthwhile obtaining the evidence of an uncle who lived abroad throughout the person's childhood. He would not be in a position to state anything useful about the matter of non-baptism. The witnesses must really be the parents, or failing them very close relatives with whom the child was brought up.

What has been said above, of course, concerns a situation within a notionally Christian context. It has already been noted that even amongst this group of people the incidence of baptism is decreasing. There are also the situations of persons who are either immigrants or those born here to parents with a Middle-Eastern or Asian background and members of those cultures which do not baptise – Muslims, Hindus, Buddhists and the like. In these situations, it is necessary to establish that the person whose non-baptism is to be established came from such a culture where baptism is not practised. In such circumstances, special provisions may well have to be made to establish, to the extent of moral certainty, that the person in question is indeed unbaptised.

Evidence is taken from these persons under oath or affirmation, and the questioning seeks to establish not merely that the witness knows that the child was not baptised, but that he can also state why not. The reason for a child not being baptised can add considerably to the likelihood, or the reverse, of the facts alleged. The questions would establish the relationship of the witness to the one alleged to be unbaptised: how close the witness was to the child; why he would have known about a baptism if one had taken place; whether the child had been in hospital, or had any serious illness; had taken part in any church activities – Sunday School, cubs, choir, etc; had worshipped in any churches; and such questions as to establish the possibility, the reasons, and likelihood of the alleged non-baptism. The petitioner is also questioned. The witnesses and the petitioner are also questioned concerning the marriage which is alleged to be non-sacramental. It is necessary to establish how it broke down – for example, whether the petitioner was the malicious cause of the breakdown. If he was, it would be very unlikely indeed that a dissolution would be granted. Where possible, the other party to the original union should be contacted and asked about the circumstances of the breakdown.

Following upon this positive evidence, a certain amount of negative evidence must be obtained. Negative evidence is obtained by conducting searches in the baptismal records of the churches in the areas where the person lived from the time of birth to the time of the marriage and even afterwards, if necessary. This involves the places where it is likely (or reasonable to believe) that the person could have been baptised. It will be appreciated that baptismal searches can never establish that a person was not baptised. They will merely establish that there is no record of a baptism in the registers of the churches searched. Moreover, this leaves open the possibility that the minister of the baptism did not enter the record of the baptism into the register. Since it is not possible to search every baptismal register everywhere, it follows that searching merely constitutes corroborative evidence of the positive testimony which has been obtained from the witnesses.

It may be thought that this type of corroborative evidence is not important. On the contrary, almost every Tribunal has had the experience where the parents of a child have stated under oath that their child was never baptised, and after careful searches, evidence of baptism is discovered. Sometimes the parents may have just forgotten or be genuinely mistaken; or other occasions it can become clear that the witnesses were deliberately lying so as to mislead the Tribunal. Obviously great care must be taken with cases such as this, so that if a dissolution is finally granted, it is clear beyond all reasonable doubt, the person concerned was never baptised and that the union was therefore not a sacrament.

The Procedure

When someone approaches a Tribunal, and wishes to submit a petition on the grounds that his or her marriage was not a sacrament, the first step taken by the Tribunal is to assist the person concerned to formulate a petition. This sets out the brief facts concerning the marriage, why it took place, why it broke down; and details concerning the alleged non-baptism. The names and addresses of witnesses, of the kind mentioned above, are also obtained. The petitioner is subsequently asked to give sworn evidence. In addition to the questions about the marriage and about the alleged non-baptism, he is also asked if he is quite clear that if the dissolution is obtained as a result of perjury any subsequent union would be null and void. The evidence is taken under oath.

Thereafter, the witnesses named, wherever they may be, are also questioned. At the same time, baptismal searches are carried out. When the evidence of the witnesses and the relevant documents, a list of which is given below, have been obtained, and the results of the baptismal searches collated, all the material is transcribed. It is then submitted to the Defender of the Bond, who examines the dossier, and sees whether all possible steps have been taken to establish the non-baptism. If he considers that more should be done to cover certain possibilities, he has the right to ask for these further enquiries to be made. It can happen that as a result of these further investigations the baptism of the person concerned is discovered. When the Defender of the Bond is satisfied that everything necessary has been done, he returns the dossier to the Tribunal with his comments on the case. The documents required a natural bond case are:

- Baptismal Certificate of the Catholic or Non-Catholic petitioner.
- Baptismal Certificate of the Catholic or non-Catholic respondent.
- Marriage Certificate of the union in question.
- Divorce Decree Absolute of the same union.
- Any dispensation from disparity of cult.
- Baptismal Certificates of children.
- Marriage Certificate of the petitioner if the petitioner has already remarried.
- Baptismal Certificate of the proposed spouse.
- Letter from the priest concerning the Catholic practice of the proposed spouse.
- Evidence of the freedom of the proposed spouse.
- Promise made by the petitioner and the proposed spouse – for example undertaking to raise any children as Catholics.

The dossier, containing the appropriate papers from the above list, together with the comments of the Defender of the Bond, is submitted to the Bishop of the diocese. He writes his 'opinion' on the case showing whether he is convinced by the evidence supplied, and stating whether in view of the merits, or otherwise, of the petitioner, he recommends the case to the Holy Father. The case and Bishop's opinion are then sent to the Congregation for the Doctrine of the Faith, where three specially appointed Commissioners and one Defender of the Bond examine the case. If the authorities are satisfied that the alleged non-baptism has been established, and that the merits of the petitioner warrant it, the case is then recommended to the Holy Father. The Pope personally grants the dissolution of the natural bond of marriage. There may be certain conditions attached to the dissolution. Occasionally the

Congregation may ask for more information, and this must be supplied before the case can go further.

This, then, is a brief outline of the procedure required for the conduct of the natural bond case. We must now deal with certain further points which arise.

The Baptism

In speaking about baptism we are of course concerned with Christian baptism – that is, with a valid baptism. Thus, for example, to say the words, 'I baptise you in the name of the Father, of the Son and of the Holy Ghost' *without* using water is regarded as an invalid baptism. Then again there are certain baptisms, so called, which are either non-trinitarian, or else make no pretence at the ceremony of Christian initiation as normally understood. Again, such would not constitute baptism in the sense in which we are here discussing it. But having said this, it will be realised at once that it may be difficult to establish that something described as a 'baptism' or 'christening' was not a valid form of the ceremony. Usually natural bond cases arise many years after the birth of the person, and hence it is not very likely that there would be evidence to demonstrate the invalidity of the baptism to the full satisfaction of the Congregation. Nonetheless, it is a factor to keep in mind, that some forms of baptism may be considered deficient.

Dissolution as a Favour

What we have been saying is that a petition for dissolution refers to what is normally regarded as a valid marriage. For this reason, whether or not the Holy Father chooses to dissolve a certain marriage is entirely a matter for his decision alone. The mere fact that a person has not been baptised does not constitute a right to the dissolution of the union in question. A variety of factors are involved, the first of which is whether the merits of the petitioner warrant the favour of the dissolution. We have already mentioned that a case will not be entertained if the petitioner has been the malicious cause of the break-down of the marriage. We can give an example of this. Henry, an unbaptised person, is married. The marriage is not as happy as it might be, nonetheless it does exist as a bond between two people. Then he meets a Catholic girl. Through his friendship with this girl, his own married relationship begins to deteriorate even further, and as a result he turns more and more to the Catholic girl for comfort in the situation in which he finds himself. Then he commits adultery with her. Not long afterwards, his wife discovers this and after some period of argument and dispute, the wife separates from, and divorces her husband. Henry becomes a Catholic, and then tries to pre-sent a petition for the dissolution of his marriage. In such a case, it is clear that Henry through neglect of his own marriage, has allowed the relationship between himself and his wife to be, broken, and the Catholic girl is proba-bly equally culpable. It is more than likely that he would not be allowed to petition for a dissolution for the pur-pose of marrying the Catholic girl. If the Holy Father were to dissolve the marriage so as to allow the two to marry, it would certainly seem as if the Church was condoning the dereliction of marital duties and obligations. This could not be allowed. Hence, it is necessary to establish as part of this type of case, that the petitioner and the person he wishes to marry were not responsible for the breakdown of the marriage. Stringent questioning on this issue may be necessary, but the ultimate aim is to establish the true facts of the breakdown of the marriage. Moreover, it must also be clear, even when the petitioner was not the cause of the breakdown of the marriage, that subsequent to the breakdown he is fulfilling his natural obligations by maintaining his wife and any children.

The next factor to be considered before the Holy Father can entertain the possibility of granting a dissolution is the *reason* for asking the favour. The basic reason for this is that the granting of the dissolution would be in favour of the faith of the Catholic party involved in the case. This is something which will be carefully evaluated both by the local Tribunal and by the Congregation in Rome.

The third consideration is the question of scandal. Obviously we have to draw a distinction here between two sorts of scandal. There is one kind which really might lead a person into sin – for example, when a child sees an older person doing something, it could well lead to the child considering this action to be in order, at least after an initial period of surprise. In this sense, scandal is the possible cause of someone sinning. On the other hand, scandal is also the term used to describe a certain surprise arising in a person due to a lack of instruction or understanding of Catholic teaching. For instance scandal could arise when someone learns that a neighbour has been granted a decree of nullity, never having realised that grounds for nullity existed. Obviously the term scandal is being used here in quite another sense.

When the Holy Father grants a dissolution of the natural bond of marriage, there might be circumstances which could lead to scandal in the proper sense of the word. For example, it might be well known that the petitioner was the malicious cause of the breakdown of his marriage. Scandal might well be caused if, as a result of the dissolution, he married the girl with whom he had committed adultery during his first marriage. In such a case, the Holy Father would not grant a dissolution. On the other hand, the petitioner may have led a most exemplary life, and it may have been his first wife who acted unjustly in the marriage, running off, for example, with another man and leaving her husband with three small children. If the necessary conditions for a dissolution of a natural bond of marriage are established, then the Holy Father might grant the dissolution, in spite of the fact that someone who was not aware of the teaching of the Church about the dissolution of non-sacramental unions might raise his eyebrows at the granting of the dissolution.

Therefore, before a petition can be sent to Rome, there must have been most careful enquiries made concerning the possibility of scandal. The Bishop must be well aware of the facts; and he must cause enquiries to be made into the matter to discover the precise situation concerning the possibility of scandal. The obvious purpose of such enquiries is to prevent harm to souls.

The Bishop is the sole judge of the local circumstances concerning the possibility of scandal arising from the granting of the dissolution. He is the one who recommends (or not) a case to Rome. It will be readily understood that the circumstances in every case are different, and that only a few people will be knowledgeable as to what the precise facts are. Frequently people assume that their case is 'like so and so's case'. If all the facts of both cases were available it is likely that the two cases are not at all similar. The position is made more difficult by the fact that the personal details of the marriages of the different parties are closely guarded secrets, and so must remain. For this reason, it is always as well to consult the local Tribunal rather than to formulate private opinions on the facts.

It has been the purpose of this book to try to describe some of the more intricate details involved in the handling of marriage cases by the Tribunals of the Church. It has not been the aim to attempt a legal treatise on the various aspects of the law, but merely to provide a short and practical manual, as an aid to those trying to understand the workings of the Church's marriage Tribunals. More detailed information can only come from personal consultation with Tribunals and canon lawyers.

Section VI

APPENDICES

Appendix I

PROCEDURE FOR NON CONSUMMATION CASES

Instruction issued by the Congregation for Sacraments
20th December, 1986: Protocol No. 1400/86

The Introduction of the Process

1 Besides the ordinary competence stipulated in the law (can.1699,§1) in particular cases, it is is possible to seek from the Congregation for the Sacraments an extension of competence, in such a way that a case may be dealt with in the place where the bulk of the evidence can be obtained, provided the Bishop of the domicile or quasi-domicile of the petitioner gives consent.

2 In cases in which there may be special difficulties – (cf can.1699,§2) *e.g.* contraceptive (sheath) inter-course, acknowledged penetration but without ejaculation, conception through absorption of semen, artificial insemination and other methods which have become possible through the means of modern medical science, the existence of children, defective human act, the danger of scandal or of economic harm related to granting this favour, and the like – the Bishop, before he directs the case to be intro-duced, should refer to the Congregation for the Sacraments, and should follow its directions.

3 If from the petition for a dispensation for an uncon-summated marriage, prudent doubt arises as to the validity of the marriage, the Bishop should either advise the spouses to proceed judicially, if one of them wishes to petition for the nullity of the

marriage, or decide to initiate a process for non-consummation, provided there appears to be a basis for this. (cf Instruction: *Dispensationis Matrimonii, I, e*).

4   As soon as a petition for dispensation has been received, the Bishop must ensure that the other party is advised, and whenever there appears to the possibility of success, an attempt should be made to persuade the parties to resolve their difficulties and to resume communal life. (cf cann. 1676, 1695).

5   The instruction of the case, whether it proceeds by way of non-consummation or by way of an action for nullity, will always be made by the Tribunal which should deal with the nullity. (cf can.1700,§2) For the instruction of this kind of case, the Bishop will commit it either to his own or to another Tribunal, or to a suitable priest, according to the law. (cf can.1700,§1).

6   A juridical expert, admitted by the Bishop according to the law (can.1701,§2) may not exercise (cf cann.1481-1490, 1678), as in a case of nullity, the role of advocate, but may assist the parties to introduce the case, with a view to the collection of proof, and in the case of a negative outcome, to advance further proof (cf can.1705,§3).

7   Whenever, in the instruction of a nullity case, on whatever grounds, genuine probable doubt emerges concerning the consummation of the marriage, the Tribunal – leaving aside whether the invalidity of the marriage is proved or not – communicates the matter to the parties. With the agreement of both, and having obtained a petition from one or the other for a dispensation from an unconsummated marriage, the Tribunal, by decree, suspends the nullity case. The instruction of the case for the dispensation is then completed and the *acta* is forwarded to the Congregation for the Sacraments, together with the petition for the dispensation, the comments of the Defender of the Bond, and the Opinions of the Tribunal and of the Bishop (cf can.1681). So far as the Opinion of the

Bishop is concerned, there is nothing to prevent him following the Opinion of his Tribunal and signing it. He also makes clear the existence of a just and proportionate cause for the granting of the dispensation and the absence of scandal amongst the faithful (cf can.1704,§1).

Conduct of the Case

8 So far as possible, evidence of credibility and probity of the parties and witnesses should be obtained from the parish priests of those persons. If such evidence is not available, other documents should be obtained by the Curia to evaluate the depositions. All these should be carefully included in the *acta*. (cf can.1572).

9 Whenever a party or a witness refuses to appear before the judge to give evidence, they can be allowed to give evidence to another priest or deacon or lay person delegated by the judge; or to make a declaration before a public notary; or in any other legitimate fashion *e.g.* by means of letter, provided the *acta* has some indication that it is genuine and authentic. (cf can. 1528).

10 A record of the absence of the parties from the Court (cf can.1592,§1,2) according to the norms of the law, should be shown in the *acta* (cf can.1509).

11 The Instructor of the case should obtain from the parties and the witnesses an oath of truthfulness before they give evidence (cf can.1532). They are then asked the questions prepared by the Instructor or the Defender (cf cann.1530, 1533) according to the prescribed method. The questioning should accord with the requirements of the law (cf can.1564).

12 The Instructor should ensure that, in the case of the interrogation of a female, a doctor is to be selected for his religious and moral qualities and gravity of years. (cf CDF Decree: *Qua Singulari:* 12th June 1942; CLD Vol.2, pp.544-551: n.6).

13   In evaluating witnesses (the number of whom is now
      no longer stipulated; i.e. witnesses *septimae manus*)
      the Instructor is to consider the criteria given in the
      law (cf can.1572), and if need be to obtain witnesses
      to the credibility of the parties. (cf can.1679).

14   Everything which would seem to assist in the proper
      instruction of the case, and which is lawful, should
      be produced. (cf can.1527,§1).

15   The Instructor should make use of one or more
      experts. (cf can.1560,§2).

16   An expert, having taken the oath (cf can.1454), in ful-
      filling his role should conform to the requirements of
      the canons. (cf can.1578,§2) The expert should be
      given the *acta* of the case and other documents and
      subsidiary papers which will enable him faithfully to
      fulfil his task. (cf can.1577,§2)

17   The judge may draw up questions to be put to the
      expert to obtain whatever further explanations
      which seem to be necessary (cf can.1578,§3).

18   A physical examination should be carried out if this
      is necessary to obtain juridical proof of non-consum-
      mation. But this examination may be omitted if, in
      the Instructor's judgement, there is already proof of
      non-consummation by means of moral arguments. It
      would not be required if from a physical examina-
      tion of the man, his incapacity to consummate
      becomes evident, and if the woman refuses a physi-
      cal examination. If the latter is the case, the woman
      should be warned of the juridical consequences of
      her refusal. (cf Decree *Qua Singulari*: nn. 1 & 4: CLD.
      Vol 2, pp.549-550).

19   The report on the physical (medical) examination
      conducted in private, should (if the instructor thinks
      fit) be placed in the *acta*, and if need be accompanied
      by medical explanations. (cf cann.1575, 1581).

20   If the experts disagree with each other, it is useful to
      submit the dispute for resolution by an even more
      eminent expert; even to one at the top of his profession.

The Conclusion of the Case

21 The Instructor in the preparation of his report (cf can.1704,§1), should draw up a summary of the whole case and add this to the *acta*.

22 The Defender of the Bond has the responsibility of proposing and expounding those points which may reasonably he advanced against the granting of the dispensation for marriage. (cf can.1432).

23 So far as the *Votum* on the case is concerned, the following points should be borne in mind:

a The Bishop should draw up the *Votum* himself. He can, however, delegate this duty by special mandate to the Vicar General or Episcopal Vicar (cf can.134,§3). If he does this, the Bishop must in some way make the *Votum* of the delegate his own, before he sends it to the Congregation for the Sacraments. (cf Reply of Code Commission of 21.2.1984.)

b Where a case is passed from the judicial to the administrative procedure (cf can.1681), a *Votum* concerning the truth of the case is to be prepared by the Bishop of the regional or inter-diocesan Tribunal, who must have conferred beforehand with the Bishop of the Petitioner, at least concerning the opportuneness of granting the dispensation. (cf Instruction S.C.Sacs: *Dispensationis Matrimonii* 7th March, 1972: II.f: CLD.Vol.7. p.995). If, however, the nullity case had been dealt with by a Diocesan Tribunal, the Votum is to be prepared by the competent Bishop.

c In the preparation of this *Votum*, the Bishop should consider the alleged fact of non-consummation and the just cause for granting the dispensation. Bearing pastoral considerations in mind in the *Votum*, he should comment upon the opportuneness of the favour, the absence of scandal or *admiratio* of the faithful or harm of any kind which could arise from the dispensation being granted; as well as the consequences of the granting of the petition in connection with the good of soul and the quieting of conscience and other such matters.

Removal of Clauses attached to the Rescript of Dispensation

24 The removal of a restrictive clause attached to the rescript lies within the competence of the Congregation for the Sacraments. Should the party who is affected by such a clause wish to enter into a new marriage, the Bishop should refer the matter to the Congregation and seek its instructions.

25 Where the removal of the restrictive clause its committed to the diocesan Bishop, the instructions given in the rescript should be followed; and the person in question should not be allowed to enter another marriage, until (by means of a medical inspection) the person's ability to perform the conjugal act has been established or a serious undertaking has been made by the person to fulfil his or her marriage obligations. (cf Instruction: *Dispensationis Matrimonii* III(a) and (b); CLD. Vol.7, p.996).

26 If in the judgement of the Congregation, further instructions needed to establish the alleged non-consummation, it will signify this to the Bishop as well as pointing out those further elements of proof which are required.

27 Although the Congregation may reply: 'From what has been produced the non-consummation has not been established', the parties always have the ability (assisted by an expert in law) to determine whether there is more information which could be proposed and added to the petition. (cf. Can.1705,§3).

Lastly, Bishops should ensure in the instruction of cases of such importance, that so far as is possible they are dealt with carefully, diligently and promptly lest useless delays work to the detriment of the parties.

20th December, 1986.   A. *Card.Mayer (Prefect)*
                              L. *Kada (Secretary)*

Congregation of the Sacraments

Notes on the procedure for non-consummated marriages issued by a Circular Letter and Norms of the S.C. Sacs on 20th December 1986 (Prot. No. 1400/86)

The following observations on certain parts of the Circular Letter and the Norms indicate the areas where there is change in the existing procedure as established in the Code and other Documents. The references to these documents are given together with the reference to the English text in *Canon Law Digest*.

1   *Competence*: (n.1) Competence in these cases is based on the provisions of can.1699,§1; but the present norms allow for this competence to be widened to include the place where the bulk of the evidence could be taken. The enlarging of competence in this way must be sought from the Congregation.

2   *Specially difficult cases*: (n.2) This gives examples of what the Code describes in general terms as 'special difficulties of a judicial or moral order' (can.1699,§2).

3   *Humano Modo*: (n.2) The Circular Letter draws attention to the requirement of the Code that marriage is regarded as consummated if intercourse takes place *humano modo*. (can.1061,§1).

The Letter says: 'It is necessary for the consummation of marriage for there to be a human act on the part of both spouses which is voluntary (*virtualiter*), and there is no violence. However psychological elements which might make the act easier or more loving are not taken into account'. The Norms said that if there is any doubt about the act being *humano modo*, then the matter must be referred to the Congregation and its instructions followed. It is to be noted that the emergence of such a doubt would more than likely only be after the commencement of the evidence stage of the case. But the requirement to refer the matter to the Congregation would still obtain.

4   *Evidence of the female*: (n.12) A doctor should be present at the interrogation of the female. (cf CDF decr. *Qua Singulari;* CLD, vol.2 pp.551 n.6).

5   *The Votum*: (n.23.c) The Norms give indications of what the *Votum* should deal with, *i.e.*, not merely the alleged fact of non-consummation, but also the opportuneness of granting the dispensation, the matter of scandal and *admiratio*; the effect of the granting of the dispensation from the point of view of the good of souls and the quieting of conscience.

6   *Removal of Restrictive Clauses:* (24) The Norms go beyond the Code by explaining the procedure for the removal of a restrictive clause which may have been imposed by the Congregation when the dispensation was granted. The matter has to be referred back to the Congregation. (cf Instr. *Dispensations Matrimonii*: III.a; CLD. vol.7, p.996).

References to Documents Relevant to Procedure

Decree of S.C.Sacs: *Catholica Doctrina* and the *Regulae servandae in processibus super matrimonio rato et non-consummato*; 7.5. 1923 in *Canon Law Digest*, vol.1, pp. 764-796.

Instruction of S.C.Sacs: *Dipensationis Matrimonii*; (7.3.1972); in *Canon Law Digest* vol. 7, pp.988-997.

Decree of CDF: *Qua Singulari*; (12.6.1942; in *Canon Law Digest*, vol.2, pp.549-551.

Appendix II

SPECIAL INSTRUCTION OF THE CONGREGATION FOR THE DOCTRINE OF THE FAITH CONCERNING THE PROCEDURE OF NATURAL BOND CASES, DATED 6 DECEMBER 1973

(Ref: SCDF prot. no. 2717/68)

Although this Instruction was issued by the Congregation for Doctrine of the Faith in the reign of Pope Paul VI it is still regarded as being in force.

As is well known, this Congregation has subjected to lengthy investigation and study the question of the dissolution of marriage in favour of the faith.

At length, after this careful investigation, His Holiness, Pope Paul VI, has approved new norms which express the conditions for the grant of the dissolution of marriage in favour of the faith whether the petitioner is baptised or converted or not.

I The following three conditions *sine qua non* are required for the valid grant of the dissolution:
  a absence of baptism in one of the spouses throughout the entire period of conjugal life;
  b non-use of marriage after baptism, if the sacrament is received by the party who was previously non baptised;
  c that the unbaptised person or the person baptised outside the Catholic Church leaves to the Catholic party the freedom and opportunity to profess his or

her own religion and to baptise and bring up the children as Catholics. This condition, in the form of a promise (*cautio*), is to be kept safely.

II   The following are required in addition:

§1 That there be no possibility of restoring conjugal life, in view of the continuing radical and incurable separation.

§2 That there be no danger of public scandal or serious wonderment from the grant of the favour.

§3 That the petitioner be shown not to have been the culpable cause of the failure of a legitimate marriage and that the Catholic party, with whom the new marriage is to be contracted or validated, was not the guilty cause of the separation of the spouses.

§4 That the second party in the prior marriage be questioned, if possible, and not be reasonably opposed to the granting of the dissolution.

§5 That the party who seeks the dissolution sees to the religious formation of any children from the prior marriage.

§6 That equitable provision be made, according to the norms of justice, for the previous spouse and any children.

§7 That the Catholic party with whom the new marriage is to be entered lives in accord with his or her baptismal promises and is concerned for the welfare of the new family.

§8 If it is a question of a catechumen with whom marriage is to be contracted, there should be moral certainty of the baptism which is to be received in the future, if the baptism itself has not taken place (which is preferable).

III The dissolution is more easily granted where there is a serious doubt concerning the validity of the marriage, arising on other grounds.

IV   It is also possible to dissolve the marriage between a Catholic and an unbaptised person which was entered into with a dispensation from the impediment of disparity of cult, provided the conditions established in nos. II and III are verified and it is established that the Catholic, because of the particular circumstances of the region, especially the small number of Catholics, could not have avoided marriage and lead a life proper to the Catholic religion in that marriage. It is necessary, in addition that this Congregation be informed concerning the public knowledge of the marriage celebrated.

V   The dissolution of a legitimate marriage entered into with a dispensation from the impediment of disparity of cult is not granted to a Catholic petitioner in order to enter a new marriage with an unbaptised person who is not converted.

VI The dissolution of a legitimate marriage which was contracted or validated after a dissolution from a previous legitimate marriage is not granted.

In order that these conditions may be properly fulfilled, new procedural norms have been drawn up, and all future processses are to be carried out in accord with them. These norms are attached to the present Instruction. With establishment of the new norms, the earlier regulations for the conduct of these processes are entirely abrogated.

Procedural Norms for the Process of Dissolution of the Bond of Marriage in Favour of the Faith

Art. 1:   The process which is to precede the granting of the favour of a dissolution of legitimate marriage is conducted by the local Ordinary who is competent in accord with the prescription of the Apostolic Letter *Causas Matrimoniales*, IV, §1, either personally or through another ecclesiastic delegated by him. The *acta* to be sent to the Holy See must contain proof of the fact of delegation or commission.

Art. 2:   Allegations must not be simply asserted but

proved in accord with the prescriptions of the canon law, either by documents or by trustworthy depositions of witnesses.

Art 3:   Both original documents and authentic copies must be certified by the Ordinary or by the delegated judge.

Art. 4:   §1 In the preparation of questions to be asked of the parties and witnesses, the services of the defender of the bond or of some other person delegated for this function in individual cases must be employed. This delegation is to be mentioned in the *acta*.

§2 Before the witnesses are questioned they must take an oath to speak the truth.

§3 The Ordinary or his delegate should ask the questions already prepared. He may add other questions which he judges appropriate for a better understanding of the matter or which are suggested by the responses already given.

When the parties or witnesses testify concerning facts not of their own knowledge, the judge should question them also concerning the reason for or the origin of their knowledge.

§4 The judge must take great care that the question and the responses be accurately transcribed by the notary and signed by the witnesses.

Art. 5:   §1 If a non-Catholic witness refuses to present himself or to testify before a Catholic priest, a document containing a deposition on the matter given by the witness before a notary public or other trustworthy person may be accepted. This is to be expressly noted in the *acta*.

§2 In order to decide whether this document is to be given credence, the Ordinary or the delegated judge should introduce sworn witnesses, especially Catholics, who know the non-Catholic witness well and are willing and able to testify to his truthfulness.

§3 The judge himself should also express his opinion concerning the credence to be given to this document.

Art. 6: §1 The absence of baptism in one of the spouses is to be demonstrated in such a way that all prudent doubt is removed.

§2 The party who says that he was [not] baptised should be questioned under oath, if possible.

§3 Moreover, witnesses and especially the parents and blood relatives of the party should be examined, as well as others, especially those who knew the party during infancy or throughout the course of his life.

§4 Witnesses are to be questioned not only concerning the absence of baptism but also concerning the circumstances which make it believable or probable that baptism was not conferred.

§5 Care should be taken to search the baptismal registers of places where the person who was said to be unbaptised lived during infancy, especially in churches which he frequented to acquire religious instruction or where the marriage was celebrated.

Art. 7: §1 If at the time the dissolution is sought the unbaptised person has already been admitted to baptism, at least a summary process must be conducted, with the intervention of the defender of the bond, concerning the non-use of marriage after reception of baptism.

§2 The party should be questioned under oath concerning the kind of contract he or she may have had with the other party after the separation and especially asked whether following baptism he or she had matrimonial relations with the other person.

§3 The other party is also to be questioned, under oath if possible, concerning the non-consummation of the marriage.

§4 In addition, witnesses, especially blood relatives and friends, are to be questioned, likewise under oath, not only concerning what has taken place after the separation of the parties and especially after the baptism, but also with regard to the probity and truthfulness of the parties, that is, concerning the credence which their testimony deserves.

Art. 8: The petitioner, if converted and baptised, should be questioned concerning the time and the intention which led him to receive baptism or to be converted.

Art. 9: §1 In the same case, the judge should question the parish priest and other priests who participated in the doctrinal instruction and in the preparation for conversion concerning the reason which led the petitioner to receive baptism.

§2 The Ordinary should never direct any petition to the Congregation for the Doctrine of the Faith unless every reasonable suspicion concerning the sincerity of conversion has been removed.

Art. 10: §1 The Ordinary or judge should question the petitioner or the witnesses concerning the reason for the separation or divorce, namely, whether the petitioner was the cause or not.

§2 The judge should include in the acts an authentic copy of the divorce decree.

Art. 11: The judge or the Ordinary should report whether the petitioner has children from the marriage or other union and how he has provided or intends to provide for their religious upbringing.

Art. 12: The judge or the Ordinary should likewise report how the petitioner will make or intends to make equitable provision for the spouse and the children if any, in accord with the laws of justice.

Art. 13: The Ordinary or judge should gather information concerning the non-Catholic party from whom he may determine whether the restoration of conjugal life can be hoped for. He should not fail to report whether the non-Catholic party has attempted a new marriage after divorce.

Art. 14: The Ordinary should report expressly whether any danger is to be feared of scandal, *admiratio*, or calumnious interpretation if the dissolution were to be granted, either among Catholics or among non-Catholics, as if the Church in practice was favourable to divorce. He should explain the circumstances which makes this danger probable in the case or exclude it.

Art. 15: The Ordinary should express the reasons which support the granting of the favour in the individual cases, at the same time always adding whether the petitioner has already attempted a new marriage in any form or is living in another union. The Ordinary should also report the fulfilment of the conditions for the grant of the favour and whether the promises mentioned in no. I, c), were given. He should transmit an authentic document, with these promises.

Art. 16: The Ordinary should send to the Congregation for the Doctrine of the Faith three copies of the petition, all the *acta*, and the information concerning which he is bound to report.

INDEX